Master the Art of Effective Communication

Proven Strategies to Enhance Your Personal and Professional Relationships

TOM ROBBINS

The presentation of the information is without contract or any type of guarantee assurance. The trademarks that are used are without any consent, and the publication of the trademark is without permission or backing by the trademark owner. All trademarks and brands within this book are for clarifying purposes only and are the owned by the owners themselves, not affiliated with this document.

Table of Contents

Chapter 1

Foundations of Effective Communication

Understanding Communication Basics

Communication is the cornerstone of human interaction, shaping our relationships and influencing our personal and professional lives. At its essence, communication is the exchange of information between individuals through a common system of symbols, signs, or behavior. Understanding the basics of communication is crucial to mastering its more complex aspects and enhancing your overall effectiveness.

Effective communication begins with the sender, the person who initiates the message. The sender must first encode the message, transforming their thoughts into words, gestures, or other symbols that can be understood by the receiver. This process of encoding is influenced by the sender's background, experiences, and perceptions, all of which shape how the message is constructed. The choice of words, tone, and body language are all critical elements that contribute to how the message will be received and interpreted.

Perception plays a significant role in communication. Each person's perception is shaped by their experiences, beliefs, and values, which act as a filter through which they interpret messages. This means that two people can receive the same message but understand it in very different ways. Being aware of this can help you tailor your communication to be more effective, by considering the perspective of your audience and anticipating how they might interpret your message.

Barriers to effective communication can arise from many sources, including physical, psychological, and semantic obstacles. Physical barriers, such as noise or distance, can impede the transmission of the message. Psychological barriers, such as stress or emotional distress, can affect both the sender's ability to convey the message clearly and the receiver's ability to interpret it accurately. Semantic barriers occur when the sender and receiver have different understandings of the words or symbols used in the message. Overcoming these barriers requires awareness and effort, such as choosing clear language, ensuring a conducive environment for communication, and being mindful of emotional and psychological states.

The communication process model provides a framework for understanding how communication occurs. This model typically includes several key components: the sender, the message, the channel, the receiver, feedback, and context. The sender initiates the communication by encoding a message and selecting a channel through which to send it. The channel can be verbal, such as speaking or writing, or nonverbal, such as gestures or facial expressions. The receiver then decodes the message, interpreting its meaning based on their own perceptions and experiences. Feedback from the receiver to the sender completes the cycle, allowing the sender to gauge whether the message was understood as intended and make any necessary adjustments.

Developing a communication mindset involves adopting attitudes and behaviors that enhance your ability to communicate effectively. This includes being open and receptive to feedback, actively listening to others, and being empathetic towards their perspectives. Active listening requires more than just hearing the words being spoken; it involves fully engaging with the speaker, understanding their message, and responding thoughtfully. Empathy, the ability to understand and share the feelings of another, is crucial for building rapport and trust in communication.

One practical way to improve your communication skills is by paying attention to your nonverbal cues. Body language, facial expressions, and eye contact can all convey powerful messages, often more so than words. For example, maintaining eye contact can demonstrate confidence and interest, while crossed arms might suggest defensiveness or disinterest. Being aware of your own nonverbal signals, as well as those of others, can help you communicate more effectively and interpret the unspoken messages in any interaction.

Another important aspect of effective communication is clarity. Clear communication is essential for ensuring that your message is understood as intended. This involves choosing your words carefully, avoiding jargon or overly complex language, and being concise. It also means organizing your thoughts before speaking or writing, so that your message is coherent and logical. Providing context and background information can also help the receiver understand the message more fully.

Feedback is a critical component of the communication process. It allows the sender to know whether their message was received and understood correctly, and it provides an opportunity for clarification if necessary. Constructive feedback should be specific, focused on behavior rather than the person, and delivered in a way that is respectful and supportive. When receiving feedback, it is important to be open and non-defensive, viewing it as an opportunity for growth and improvement.

In professional settings, effective communication is essential for teamwork, productivity, and overall success. Clear and open communication can prevent misunderstandings, resolve conflicts, and foster a positive work environment. It is important to communicate expectations clearly, provide regular updates, and encourage open dialogue among team members. Active listening and empathy are particularly important in a professional context, as they can help build strong working relationships and create a culture of mutual respect and collaboration.

In personal relationships, effective communication is the foundation of trust and intimacy. It allows individuals to express their needs, desires, and concerns, and to understand those of their partners. Open and honest communication can prevent misunderstandings and conflicts, and help to resolve them when they do arise. It is important to communicate with empathy and sensitivity, being mindful of the other person's feelings and perspectives.

Developing a communication mindset also involves being aware of the impact of cultural differences on communication. Different cultures have distinct norms and practices related to communication, which can influence how messages are sent and received. For example, some cultures value directness and clarity, while others may prioritize harmony and indirect communication. Understanding these cultural nuances can help you navigate cross-cultural interactions more effectively and avoid potential misunderstandings.

The Role of Perception in Communication

Perception is the lens through which we view the world, and it plays a crucial role in communication. It shapes how we interpret messages, influences our interactions with others, and affects the overall effectiveness of our communication. Understanding the role of perception in communication can help you become more aware of how your own perceptions influence your interactions and how to better navigate the perceptions of others.

Imagine you are at a meeting where a colleague presents a new idea. Depending on your previous experiences with this colleague, your perception of their competence, and even your mood that day, you might view their idea as brilliant, mediocre, or flawed. This subjective interpretation is a product of perception. Our brains constantly filter and interpret sensory information, creating a personalized view of reality. This means that two people can experience the same event and come away with entirely different understandings.

One key aspect of perception in communication is selective perception, where individuals focus on certain aspects of a message while ignoring others. This can happen consciously or unconsciously. For example, if you have a positive relationship with someone, you are more likely to focus on their positive attributes and overlook their faults. Conversely, if you have a negative relationship, you might only see their shortcomings and ignore their strengths. Being aware of selective perception can help you strive for a more balanced view, ensuring that you consider the full context of a message rather than just the parts that confirm your existing beliefs.

Perception is also influenced by psychological factors such as emotions, attitudes, and expectations. Emotions can significantly skew perception. When you are angry or stressed, you might misinterpret neutral comments as hostile. Similarly, if you are in a good mood, you might overlook subtle signs of discontent or disagreement. Attitudes and expectations shape perception by creating a mental framework through which we interpret information. For instance, if you expect a conversation to be difficult, you might enter it with a defensive mindset, which in turn affects how you perceive the other person's words and actions.

Cultural background plays a significant role in shaping perception. Culture affects what we pay attention to, how we interpret those observations, and how we respond. For example, in some cultures, direct eye contact is seen as a sign of confidence and honesty, while in others, it can be perceived as rude or confrontational. Understanding cultural differences in perception can help you navigate cross-cultural communications more effectively. It fosters greater empathy and reduces the likelihood of misunderstandings.

Perception can also lead to various biases that impact communication. One common bias is the halo effect, where our overall impression of a person influences how we perceive their specific traits or behaviors. If you perceive someone as generally competent, you might overlook their mistakes or attribute them to external factors. Conversely, the horn effect means that if you have a negative overall impression, you might view their actions more critically. Recognizing these biases can help you strive for a more objective and fair assessment of others.

Another important concept is attribution theory, which examines how people explain the causes of behavior. We tend to attribute our own successes to internal factors (like effort and ability) and our failures to external factors (such as bad luck or difficult circumstances). In contrast, we often attribute others' successes to external factors and their failures to internal ones. This bias, known as the fundamental attribution error, can lead to misunderstandings and conflict in communication. By being aware of this tendency, you can try to consider external factors when evaluating others' behavior, leading to more compassionate and effective communication.

Perception also plays a role in nonverbal communication. Body language, facial expressions, and tone of voice are all subject to interpretation, and our perceptions can significantly influence how we decode these nonverbal cues. For instance, a smile can be perceived as genuine or forced depending on the context and our relationship with the person. Misinterpreting nonverbal signals can lead to misunderstandings, so it is crucial to consider the context and look for congruence between verbal and nonverbal messages.

One practical way to manage the impact of perception in communication is to seek clarification. When you are unsure about someone's message or intent, ask questions to confirm your understanding. Phrases like "Can you explain what you mean?" or "I want to make sure I understand your point correctly" can help clear up potential misinterpretations. This not only ensures you have accurately received the message but also shows the other person that you value their perspective and are making an effort to understand them.

Another strategy is to practice empathy, which involves putting yourself in the other person's shoes and trying to see the situation from their perspective. Empathy can help you better understand the factors influencing their perception and communication. It can also reduce the likelihood of conflict and build stronger, more positive relationships. To practice empathy, pay close attention to the other person's verbal and nonverbal cues, and try to imagine how they might be feeling and what might be motivating their behavior.

Self-awareness is also crucial for managing perception in communication. By reflecting on your own biases, emotions, and attitudes, you can become more aware of how they influence your perceptions and interactions. Regular self-reflection can help you identify patterns in your responses and perceptions, allowing you to adjust your communication strategies accordingly. For instance, if you notice that you tend to become defensive when receiving feedback, you can work on developing a more open and receptive attitude.

Barriers to Effective Communication

Barriers to effective communication can significantly hinder our ability to connect and share information with others. These barriers can arise from various sources, ranging from personal biases and cultural differences to environmental factors and emotional states. Understanding these obstacles is crucial for improving our communication skills and fostering more meaningful interactions.

One of the most common barriers to effective communication is language differences. Even when people speak the same language, regional dialects, jargon, and industry-specific terminology can create confusion. For instance, a software engineer might use technical terms that are unfamiliar to someone outside the tech industry, leading to misunderstandings. To overcome this barrier, it is essential to be mindful of your audience's background and adjust your language accordingly. Simplifying your message, avoiding jargon, and explaining complex terms can help bridge the gap.

Cultural differences also play a significant role in communication barriers. Each culture has its own set of norms, values, and communication styles, which can affect how messages are sent and received. For example, in some cultures, direct eye contact is a sign of confidence and honesty, while in others, it can be perceived as disrespectful or aggressive. Similarly, high-context cultures rely heavily on nonverbal cues and the context of the conversation, whereas low-context cultures prioritize explicit verbal communication. Being aware of these cultural differences and making an effort to understand and respect them can improve cross-cultural communication.

Another barrier to effective communication is emotional interference. Strong emotions such as anger, frustration, or anxiety can cloud judgment and impede the clarity of messages. When emotions run high, people are more likely to misinterpret others' words or react defensively. For instance, during a heated argument, individuals might focus more on winning the argument rather than understanding the other person's perspective. To manage emotional barriers, it is important to remain calm, practice active listening, and take breaks if needed to cool down before continuing the conversation.

Perceptual barriers also play a crucial role in communication breakdowns. Our perceptions are influenced by past experiences, beliefs, and biases, which can lead us to interpret messages differently than intended. For example, if you have had negative experiences with a particular colleague, you might perceive their feedback as criticism, even if it is constructive. Being aware of your own biases and striving to approach conversations with an open mind can help mitigate perceptual barriers.

Physical barriers, such as environmental noise and poor acoustics, can also interfere with effective communication. Imagine trying to have a conversation in a noisy restaurant or during a loud construction project. These distractions can make it difficult to hear and understand the speaker, leading to miscommunication. To overcome physical barriers, choose a quiet and comfortable setting for important conversations, and use clear and concise language to minimize misunderstandings.

Technological barriers are increasingly relevant in today's digital age. While technology has made communication more accessible, it has also introduced new challenges. Poor internet connections, malfunctioning equipment, and unfamiliarity with digital platforms can hinder effective communication. For instance, a virtual meeting might be disrupted by audio issues or participants struggling to use the software. To address technological barriers, ensure that all participants are comfortable with the tools being used, provide training if necessary, and have backup plans in case of technical difficulties.

Another significant barrier to effective communication is psychological noise, which refers to internal distractions such as personal worries, stress, or preoccupations. When your mind is occupied with personal concerns, it is challenging to fully engage in a conversation and understand the other person's message. For example, if you are worried about an upcoming deadline, you might miss important details in a meeting. To reduce psychological noise, practice mindfulness techniques, prioritize self-care, and try to be fully present during interactions.

Semantic barriers arise from differences in the meanings of words and symbols. Even within the same language, words can have multiple meanings or connotations that vary based on context and individual interpretation. For example, the word "fine" can mean satisfactory, good, or even a monetary penalty, depending on the context. Misunderstandings can occur when people attach different meanings to the same words. To overcome semantic barriers, aim for clarity and precision in your language, and ask for feedback to ensure your message is understood as intended.

Listening barriers are another common obstacle in effective communication. Active listening requires full attention and engagement, but various factors can impede our ability to listen effectively. Distractions, preconceived notions, and selective hearing can all contribute to poor listening. For instance, if you are distracted by your phone during a conversation, you might miss crucial information. Improving listening skills involves making a conscious effort to focus on the speaker, avoiding interruptions, and providing feedback to demonstrate understanding.

One practical strategy to overcome communication barriers is to practice empathy. Empathy involves putting yourself in the other person's shoes and trying to understand their perspective and emotions. By empathizing with others, you can build rapport and create a more supportive communication environment. For example, if a colleague is upset about a project setback, acknowledging their feelings and offering support can help them feel heard and understood, leading to a more productive conversation.

Feedback is another valuable tool for overcoming communication barriers. Providing and receiving feedback helps clarify messages, correct misunderstandings, and improve future interactions. Constructive feedback should be specific, focused on behavior rather than personal attributes, and delivered in a supportive manner. For instance, instead of saying, "You're always late with your reports," you could say, "I've noticed the last few reports have been submitted after the deadline. Is there something we can do to help manage the timeline better?" This approach fosters a problem-solving mindset and encourages open dialogue.

The Communication Process Model

Understanding the communication process model is essential for anyone seeking to enhance their communication skills. This model provides a framework that explains how information is transmitted from one person to another, highlighting the key components and stages involved. By breaking down the process into manageable parts, we can identify potential pitfalls and improve the clarity and effectiveness of our interactions.

The communication process begins with the sender, who is responsible for crafting the message. This stage involves encoding, where the sender translates their thoughts, ideas, or feelings into a form that can be conveyed to the recipient. Encoding can take various forms, such as spoken or written words, body language, or visual images. The sender must consider the audience and context to choose the most appropriate method of encoding. For example, a manager delivering performance feedback might opt for a face-to-face meeting to convey empathy and ensure clarity.

Once the message is encoded, it is transmitted through a chosen channel. Channels can be verbal, nonverbal, written, or digital, and each has its own strengths and weaknesses. Verbal communication, such as a phone call or in-person conversation, allows for immediate feedback and clarification. Written communication, like emails or reports, provides a record of the message but lacks the immediacy of verbal interactions. Digital channels, including social media and video conferencing, offer convenience and reach but can be susceptible to technical issues. Selecting the appropriate channel is crucial to ensuring the message is received as intended.

After transmission, the message reaches the receiver, who is tasked with decoding it. Decoding involves interpreting and making sense of the encoded message. The receiver's ability to decode accurately depends on their knowledge, experience, and context. Misunderstandings can occur if the receiver misinterprets the sender's words or nonverbal cues. For instance, reading a sarcastic comment in an email without the accompanying tone of voice can lead to confusion or offense. To facilitate effective decoding, the sender should strive for clear and unambiguous language, while the receiver should actively engage in the process and seek clarification if needed.

Feedback is a critical component of the communication process model. It serves as a response from the receiver back to the sender, indicating whether the message was understood as intended. Feedback can be verbal or nonverbal and may include questions, comments, or body language. Effective feedback helps close the communication loop, ensuring that both parties are aligned. For example, in a team meeting, a project update might be followed by questions and suggestions, allowing the sender to gauge the team's understanding and address any concerns.

Noise is an inevitable element that can disrupt the communication process at any stage. Noise refers to any interference that distorts or obstructs the transmission and reception of the message. It can be physical, such as background noise during a phone call, or psychological, like preconceived notions and biases that cloud interpretation. Environmental factors, such as poor lighting or uncomfortable seating, can also contribute to noise. Minimizing noise involves creating a conducive environment for communication and being mindful of potential distractions. For instance, choosing a quiet location for important discussions can help reduce physical noise, while fostering an open-minded attitude can mitigate psychological noise.

Context plays a significant role in shaping the communication process. Context encompasses the situational, cultural, and relational factors that influence how messages are sent, received, and interpreted. For example, cultural norms can dictate appropriate communication styles and behaviors, while the nature of the relationship between sender and receiver can affect the tone and formality of the interaction. Understanding the context allows communicators to tailor their approach to suit the specific circumstances. Acknowledging and respecting cultural differences, for instance, can enhance cross-cultural communication and prevent misunderstandings.

Effective communication also relies on the competence of both the sender and the receiver. Communication competence involves a combination of knowledge, skills, and attitudes that enable individuals to communicate effectively and appropriately. This includes being aware of communication principles, possessing the ability to encode and decode messages accurately, and demonstrating a willingness to engage in meaningful interactions. Continuous learning and practice can enhance communication competence, enabling individuals to navigate complex communication scenarios with confidence.

Active listening is a vital skill within the communication process model. It involves fully concentrating, understanding, responding, and remembering what is being said. Active listening goes beyond hearing words; it requires paying attention to nonverbal cues, asking clarifying questions, and providing feedback. This skill fosters mutual understanding and helps prevent miscommunication. For example, during a conflict resolution session, active listening can help each party feel heard and valued, paving the way for a constructive dialogue.

Empathy is another crucial element that enhances the communication process. Empathy involves understanding and sharing the feelings of others, which can build rapport and trust. By putting themselves in the other person's shoes, communicators can respond more thoughtfully and considerately. For instance, a teacher addressing a student's struggles can show empathy by acknowledging their challenges and offering support, thereby creating a supportive and encouraging environment.

Nonverbal communication significantly impacts the communication process and includes gestures, facial expressions, posture, and eye contact. These cues can reinforce or contradict verbal messages, influencing how the message is perceived. For example, a warm smile and open body language can enhance the perception of friendliness and openness during a conversation, while crossed arms and averted eyes might signal disinterest or defensiveness. Being aware of and intentionally using nonverbal signals can strengthen the message and ensure that it is received as intended. Similarly, paying attention to the nonverbal cues of others can provide additional context and insight into their true feelings and attitudes.

Developing a Communication Mindset

Developing a communication mindset is crucial for anyone aiming to enhance their interpersonal skills and build more effective relationships. A communication mindset is not just about the mechanics of speaking and listening but also involves a deeper, more reflective approach to how we engage with others. It requires an understanding of our own communication habits, the ability to empathize with others, and a commitment to continuous improvement.

The foundation of a communication mindset begins with self-awareness. This involves recognizing your own communication strengths and weaknesses. Self-awareness can be cultivated through reflection and feedback from others. For example, you might notice that you tend to interrupt others during conversations. Acknowledging this habit is the first step towards changing it. Similarly, feedback from colleagues or friends can provide insights into how your communication style is perceived and areas where you might improve.

Empathy is another cornerstone of a communication mindset. Empathy involves understanding and sharing the feelings of others. When you empathize with someone, you are better able to see things from their perspective, which can significantly enhance your ability to communicate effectively. For instance, if a co-worker seems upset during a meeting, an empathetic approach would involve asking them about their concerns and offering support, rather than ignoring their emotional state. This not only helps in resolving the immediate issue but also builds trust and rapport over time.

Active listening is a critical skill in developing a communication mindset. Active listening means fully concentrating on what the speaker is saying, rather than just passively hearing their words. It involves paying attention to both verbal and nonverbal cues, such as tone of voice, facial expressions, and body language. Techniques like nodding, maintaining eye contact, and providing verbal affirmations can demonstrate that you are engaged and interested in the conversation. Additionally, asking open-ended questions can encourage the speaker to elaborate and share more of their thoughts and feelings.

Another important aspect of a communication mindset is adaptability. Different situations and audiences require different communication approaches. For example, the way you communicate with a close friend will likely differ from how you interact with a business client. Adapting your communication style to fit the context shows respect for the other person and increases the likelihood of a successful exchange. This might involve adjusting your language, tone, or even the medium of communication to suit the specific needs of the situation.

Clarity and conciseness are essential components of effective communication. Being clear and concise helps to ensure that your message is understood as intended. This involves organizing your thoughts before speaking, avoiding jargon or overly complex language, and getting to the point without unnecessary digressions. For example, when giving instructions to a team, clearly outline the steps involved and the expected outcomes, rather than overwhelming them with too much information at once. This not only makes your communication more effective but also shows that you value the other person's time and attention.

Nonverbal communication also plays a significant role in developing a communication mindset. Nonverbal cues such as gestures, posture, and facial expressions can reinforce or contradict what you are saying. Being aware of your own nonverbal signals and interpreting those of others can enhance your ability to communicate effectively. For instance, maintaining an open posture and making eye contact can convey confidence and attentiveness, while crossed arms and averted gaze might suggest defensiveness or disinterest. By aligning your nonverbal communication with your verbal messages, you can create a more cohesive and trustworthy interaction.

Feedback is a vital element in the continuous improvement of your communication skills. Constructive feedback helps you understand how your communication is perceived and where you can make adjustments. Seeking feedback from trusted colleagues, friends, or mentors can provide valuable insights. When receiving feedback, it's important to remain open and non-defensive, focusing on the opportunity for growth rather than taking it personally. Similarly, providing feedback to others should be done thoughtfully and respectfully, focusing on specific behaviors and offering suggestions for improvement.

Mindfulness is another powerful tool in developing a communication mindset. Mindfulness involves being fully present in the moment, which can enhance your ability to listen and respond effectively. Practicing mindfulness can help reduce distractions and improve your focus during conversations. Techniques such as deep breathing, pausing before responding, and being conscious of your own emotional state can help you remain centered and engaged. This not only improves the quality of your interactions but also helps manage stress and prevent misunderstandings.

Building a communication mindset also entails a commitment to lifelong learning. Communication is a dynamic skill that can always be improved. Engaging in activities such as reading books on communication, attending workshops, or participating in public speaking groups can provide new insights and techniques. Additionally, observing effective communicators and learning from their approaches can inspire you to refine your own skills. For example, watching how a skilled negotiator handles a difficult discussion can offer practical strategies that you can apply in your own interactions.

Emotional intelligence (EI) is closely linked to a communication mindset. EI involves the ability to recognize, understand, and manage your own emotions, as well as those of others. High emotional intelligence can enhance your communication by helping you navigate complex social situations and respond appropriately to emotional cues. For instance, if you notice a colleague is stressed during a project deadline, your ability to empathize and offer support can alleviate tension and foster a more cooperative working environment. Developing emotional intelligence requires practice and reflection. You can start by paying attention to your emotional responses in various situations and considering how they affect your communication. Additionally, learning to read and respond to the emotions of others can significantly improve your interpersonal interactions.

Chapter 2

Verbal Communication Skills

The Power of Words

Words hold immense power. They shape our thoughts, influence our emotions, and drive our actions. Understanding the impact of words can transform the way we communicate, helping us to be more persuasive, empathetic, and effective in our interactions. This chapter delves into the various aspects of the power of words and provides practical guidance on how to harness this power to improve your communication skills.

The first step in appreciating the power of words is recognizing their ability to influence our perceptions. Words can frame our understanding of situations and people. For example, consider the difference between describing someone as "determined" versus "stubborn." Both words might refer to a similar behavior, but "determined" carries a positive connotation, suggesting perseverance and strength, while "stubborn" implies inflexibility and obstinance. By choosing our words carefully, we can shape the narrative in a way that aligns with our intentions and values.

Words also have the power to evoke emotions. They can comfort, inspire, anger, or hurt. Understanding this emotional impact is crucial for effective communication. For instance, during a conflict, using words that validate the other person's feelings can help de-escalate the situation. Phrases like "I understand why you feel that way" or "Your feelings are valid" can create a sense of empathy and openness, making it easier to resolve differences. Conversely, words that dismiss or belittle can exacerbate tensions and lead to further misunderstandings.

Storytelling is a powerful technique that leverages the emotional impact of words. By weaving facts and messages into a narrative, you can make your communication more engaging and memorable. Stories resonate because they tap into our innate love for narrative structures, transporting us into different experiences and perspectives. For example, instead of presenting dry statistics about the benefits of teamwork, sharing a story about a successful team project can illustrate the point more vividly and persuasively. This approach not only captures attention but also fosters a deeper connection with your audience.

The power of words extends to self-talk as well. The words we use to describe ourselves and our experiences can significantly affect our self-perception and mindset. Positive self-talk can boost confidence and resilience, while negative self-talk can undermine our abilities and motivation. Consider the difference between saying "I can't do this" versus "I haven't figured this out yet." The former is a definitive statement that closes off possibilities, while the latter acknowledges the challenge but leaves room for growth and learning. By consciously choosing empowering words in our self-talk, we can cultivate a more positive and proactive mindset.

Effective communication also involves understanding the impact of tone and delivery. The same words can convey different meanings depending on how they are said. A friendly tone can make a request seem like a favor, while a harsh tone can make it feel like a command. Paying attention to your tone and delivery is essential for ensuring that your words are received as intended. This is particularly important in written communication, where tone can be harder to convey. Using punctuation, emojis, or clarifying phrases can help ensure your message is interpreted correctly.

Nonverbal cues can reinforce or contradict the words we use. Body language, facial expressions, and gestures all play a role in how our words are perceived. For example, saying "I'm fine" while frowning and crossing your arms sends a mixed message that can lead to confusion or mistrust. Aligning your nonverbal cues with your verbal messages creates a more coherent and trustworthy communication. Practice being mindful of your nonverbal signals and how they complement your words to enhance your overall communication effectiveness.

Context is another critical factor in the power of words. The same words can have different meanings depending on the situation and the relationship between the communicators. For instance, a joke that is appropriate among friends might be inappropriate in a professional setting. Being aware of the context and adjusting your language accordingly shows respect and sensitivity. It helps ensure that your words are appropriate and effective for the given situation.

Listening is an often-overlooked aspect of the power of words. Effective communication is not just about speaking well but also about listening actively. When you listen attentively, you can better understand the other person's perspective and respond more thoughtfully. Active listening involves not just hearing the words but also paying attention to the underlying emotions and intentions. Techniques like paraphrasing, asking clarifying questions, and providing feedback can demonstrate that you are engaged and value the other person's input. This creates a more balanced and reciprocal communication dynamic.

The power of words is also evident in their ability to persuade and influence. Persuasive communication involves using words strategically to shape opinions and motivate actions. Understanding principles of persuasion, such as ethos (credibility), pathos (emotion), and logos (logic), can help you craft more compelling messages. For example, when trying to persuade a colleague to support a new initiative, you might highlight your expertise and experience (ethos), appeal to their values and emotions (pathos), and present logical arguments and evidence (logos). Combining these elements can create a more persuasive and convincing message.

Words can also empower and uplift others. Compliments, encouragement, and expressions of gratitude can have a profound impact on someone's day and overall self-esteem. Taking the time to acknowledge someone's efforts or achievements can bolster their confidence and foster a positive environment. For instance, telling a team member, "Your presentation was incredibly insightful and well-delivered," not only makes them feel appreciated but also reinforces positive behaviors and skills. Regularly practicing this form of positive reinforcement can contribute to a more motivated and cohesive team.

Enhancing Vocabulary for Better Communication

Vocabulary is the cornerstone of effective communication. It is the tool we use to express our thoughts, convey emotions, and engage with others. Enhancing one's vocabulary is not just about learning new words; it's about understanding how to use them in context to improve clarity and precision in communication. This chapter aims to provide practical strategies and techniques for enhancing vocabulary, making communication more impactful and engaging.

A rich vocabulary allows for more precise and nuanced expression. Imagine trying to describe a beautiful sunset. With a limited vocabulary, you might simply say, "The sunset is pretty." While this conveys a basic idea, it lacks depth. With an enhanced vocabulary, you might say, "The sunset is a breathtaking symphony of colors, with hues of orange, pink, and purple blending seamlessly into the horizon." The latter paints a more vivid picture, engaging the listener's imagination and emotions.

One of the most effective ways to enhance vocabulary is through reading. Diverse reading materials expose you to a wide range of words and contexts. Fiction, non-fiction, newspapers, and scientific journals each offer unique vocabularies. For instance, reading a novel might introduce you to descriptive and emotive language, while a scientific article can expand your technical and academic vocabulary. Aim to read a variety of genres and subjects to build a well-rounded vocabulary.

As you encounter new words, it's essential to actively engage with them. Simply reading a word is not enough; you must understand its meaning, pronunciation, and usage. One effective technique is to keep a vocabulary journal. Whenever you come across an unfamiliar word, write it down along with its definition, a sentence using the word, and any synonyms or antonyms. Review your journal regularly to reinforce your learning and retention.

Incorporating new words into your everyday speech and writing is crucial for internalizing them. Challenge yourself to use newly learned words in conversations, emails, or social media posts. This practice not only reinforces your memory but also helps you become more comfortable with the words. For example, instead of saying, "I'm very happy," you might say, "I'm ecstatic." This not only enhances your vocabulary but also makes your communication more engaging and specific.

Another effective strategy for enhancing your vocabulary is to learn word roots, prefixes, and suffixes. Understanding the building blocks of words can help you decipher the meanings of unfamiliar words. For instance, knowing that the prefix "bio-" means "life" and the suffix "-logy" means "study of" helps you understand that "biology" is the study of life. This knowledge can also help you recognize and understand related words, such as "biography" (a written account of someone's life) or "biodegradable" (capable of being decomposed by living organisms).

Synonyms and antonyms are also valuable tools for enhancing vocabulary. Learning multiple words that have similar or opposite meanings can help you choose the most precise word for any situation. For example, instead of repeatedly using the word "good," you can use synonyms like "excellent," "superb," or "outstanding" depending on the context. Likewise, knowing antonyms can help you better understand and describe contrasts. For example, the antonyms of "happy" include "sad," "miserable," and "unhappy," each with its own nuance.

Engaging in word games and activities can also be a fun and effective way to enhance vocabulary. Crossword puzzles, word searches, and Scrabble are excellent tools for learning new words and reinforcing existing knowledge. Additionally, apps and online platforms offer interactive vocabulary-building exercises that can be tailored to your skill level and interests. These activities make learning new words enjoyable and can be done in short, manageable sessions.

Contextual learning is another powerful method for enhancing vocabulary. Instead of memorizing lists of words in isolation, learn new words in the context of sentences and stories. This approach helps you understand how words function in real-life communication. For example, reading a sentence like "The cacophony of the bustling city was overwhelming" not only teaches you the word "cacophony" but also how it is used to describe a loud, chaotic noise. Contextual learning aids in retention and makes it easier to recall words when you need them.

Engaging in conversations with people who have a strong vocabulary can also enhance your own. Pay attention to the words they use and ask for clarification if you encounter unfamiliar terms. Not only does this expand your vocabulary, but it also improves your listening skills and understanding of different communication styles. Surrounding yourself with articulate individuals encourages you to elevate your own language use.

Language learning isn't limited to English. Exploring other languages can provide insights into word origins and enhance your understanding of English vocabulary. Many English words are derived from Latin, Greek, French, and other languages. For example, the word "television" comes from the Greek "tele" (far) and the Latin "visio" (sight). Understanding these roots can help you make connections between words and expand your vocabulary across multiple languages.

Using technology to your advantage can also facilitate vocabulary enhancement. There are numerous apps and online resources designed specifically to help you build your vocabulary. These tools often provide interactive exercises, quizzes, and personalized learning plans. Apps like Anki or Quizlet allow you to create digital flashcards for new words and review them regularly. Websites like Vocabulary.com offer comprehensive word lists, definitions, and usage examples. Leveraging these technological resources can make your vocabulary-building efforts more structured and efficient.

Tone and Clarity in Speech

Tone and clarity are essential elements in effective speech, shaping how your message is received and understood. The tone of your speech conveys your attitude and emotions, while clarity ensures that your message is precise and easily comprehensible. Mastering these aspects can significantly impact your ability to communicate effectively, whether in professional settings, social interactions, or public speaking engagements.

Imagine attending a conference where the speaker's tone is monotonous and their message is muddled. Despite the importance of the topic, the lack of engaging tone and clear articulation can make it difficult for the audience to stay focused and grasp the content. Conversely, a speaker with a dynamic tone and clear, concise language can captivate the audience, making the information accessible and memorable.

One of the first steps to improving tone in speech is to understand the different types of tones and their appropriate contexts. A formal tone is often used in professional or academic settings, characterized by a serious, respectful, and objective manner. For instance, when presenting a business proposal, your tone should be confident, assertive, and focused on facts. On the other hand, an informal tone is more casual and personal, suitable for conversations with friends or family. It's essential to match your tone to the situation to ensure your message is received as intended.

To develop a versatile tone, practice varying your pitch, pace, and volume. A dynamic pitch can help emphasize key points and convey emotions, while a steady pace prevents your speech from becoming monotonous. Adjusting your volume according to the setting and audience size ensures everyone can hear you without straining. For example, when telling a story, raising your pitch slightly and speaking more slowly can build suspense, while lowering your pitch and speaking faster can convey excitement.

Pausing strategically can also enhance your tone and clarity. Pauses give your audience time to process information and can emphasize important points. For instance, pausing after a crucial statement allows the weight of your words to sink in, making them more impactful. Additionally, pauses can give you a moment to collect your thoughts, ensuring that your speech remains coherent and focused.

Clarity in speech involves not only the choice of words but also the structure and delivery of your message. Using simple, straightforward language helps eliminate ambiguity and makes your message more accessible. Avoid jargon, slang, or overly complex vocabulary unless you are certain your audience is familiar with it. For example, instead of saying, "We need to synergize our operational strategies to optimize our ROI," you might say, "We need to work together to improve our profits."

Organizing your speech logically is also crucial for clarity. Begin with a clear introduction that outlines the main points you will cover. This helps set the stage for your audience and provides a roadmap for your speech. Each main point should be distinct and supported by relevant examples or evidence. Transition smoothly between points to maintain a cohesive flow. Conclude with a summary that reinforces your key messages and provides a clear call to action if applicable.

Pronunciation and articulation are fundamental to clear speech. Mispronouncing words or speaking unclearly can confuse your audience and undermine your credibility. Practice difficult words and phrases beforehand, and consider recording yourself to identify areas for improvement. Speaking at a moderate pace allows you to articulate each word clearly, reducing the risk of slurring or mumbling. If you tend to speak quickly, consciously slow down to ensure your audience can follow along.

Non-verbal communication also plays a significant role in tone and clarity. Your body language, facial expressions, and gestures can reinforce or contradict your spoken words. Maintaining eye contact with your audience conveys confidence and helps establish a connection. Open and relaxed body language makes you appear approachable and trustworthy. Gestures can emphasize key points, but avoid overusing them, as this can be distracting. For example, a simple hand gesture to highlight an important point can make your speech more engaging and memorable.

Feedback is invaluable for improving tone and clarity in speech. Seek constructive criticism from trusted colleagues, friends, or mentors. They can provide insights into how your tone and clarity are perceived and suggest areas for improvement. Additionally, consider joining a public speaking group or taking a communication course to refine your skills. Regular practice and feedback are essential for continuous improvement.

Adapting your tone and clarity to your audience is another crucial aspect of effective speech. Consider the demographics, cultural background, and expectations of your audience. Tailoring your speech to their needs and preferences can make your message more relatable and impactful. For example, when speaking to a group of young professionals, you might adopt a more energetic and informal tone, whereas a more formal and measured tone might be appropriate for a senior executive audience.

Listening is just as important as speaking when it comes to effective communication. Active listening helps you understand your audience's reactions and adjust your tone and clarity accordingly. Pay attention to verbal and non-verbal cues, such as nodding, facial expressions, or questions. These signals can indicate whether your audience is engaged and understanding your message. Responding to their feedback in real-time can enhance your speech and ensure your message resonates.

Storytelling is a powerful tool for enhancing tone and clarity in speech. Stories create a connection with the audience, making your message more relatable and memorable. When telling a story, ensure it is relevant to your topic and audience. Use vivid language and descriptive details to paint a picture in the listener's mind. For example, instead of simply stating that a project was challenging, you might describe the obstacles faced and the creative solutions your team implemented to overcome them. This approach not only engages your audience but also provides concrete examples that reinforce your message.

Active Listening Techniques

Active listening is a powerful communication skill that goes beyond merely hearing words; it involves fully engaging with the speaker, understanding their message, and responding thoughtfully. This practice not only enhances personal and professional relationships but also fosters trust, reduces misunderstandings, and promotes effective problem-solving. Embracing active listening techniques can transform your interactions, making your communication more meaningful and impactful.

Imagine a scenario where a colleague is sharing their frustrations about a challenging project. Instead of just nodding and waiting for your turn to speak, active listening requires you to focus entirely on their words, body language, and emotions. This level of attentiveness shows genuine interest and empathy, encouraging the speaker to open up and share more freely. By honing your active listening skills, you can create a supportive environment where others feel valued and understood.

One critical aspect of active listening is providing undivided attention. This means setting aside distractions, such as phones or laptops, and giving the speaker your full focus. Maintaining eye contact, nodding occasionally, and using facial expressions to show interest can all signal that you are engaged. For example, when a friend is recounting a personal story, leaning slightly forward and maintaining eye contact can demonstrate that you are fully present and invested in their narrative.

Reflective listening, a key component of active listening, involves paraphrasing or summarizing what the speaker has said to confirm understanding. This technique not only shows that you are paying attention but also helps clarify any potential misunderstandings. For instance, if a team member expresses concerns about a project's timeline, you might respond with, "It sounds like you're worried about meeting the deadline due to the current workload. Is that correct?" This approach ensures that both parties are on the same page and can address any issues more effectively.

Asking open-ended questions is another essential active listening technique. These questions encourage the speaker to elaborate on their thoughts and feelings, providing deeper insights into their perspective. Instead of asking yes-or-no questions, which can limit the conversation, try asking questions that begin with "how," "what," or "why." For example, if a coworker mentions a challenging aspect of their job, you might ask, "What specific challenges are you facing, and how do they impact your work?" This invites a more comprehensive response and demonstrates your genuine interest in their experiences.

Empathy plays a crucial role in active listening. It involves understanding and sharing the feelings of the speaker, which can create a stronger connection and foster trust. Empathetic listening requires you to put yourself in the speaker's shoes and consider their emotions and perspectives. For example, if a friend is upset about a personal issue, acknowledging their feelings by saying, "I can see that this situation is really tough for you," can validate their emotions and show that you care.

Silence is a powerful yet often overlooked aspect of active listening. Allowing moments of silence gives the speaker time to think and process their thoughts, which can lead to more meaningful and reflective responses. It also shows that you are patient and willing to give them space to express themselves fully. For instance, if someone pauses while sharing their thoughts, resist the urge to fill the silence and instead give them the time they need to continue at their own pace.

Non-verbal cues are integral to active listening. Your body language, facial expressions, and gestures can all convey attentiveness and understanding. Open body language, such as uncrossed arms and a relaxed posture, can make you appear more approachable and engaged. Mirroring the speaker's expressions subtly can also create a sense of rapport and empathy. For example, if the speaker is smiling while sharing a positive experience, responding with a smile can reinforce a connection and show that you share their enthusiasm.

Providing feedback is another important aspect of active listening. Offering thoughtful and relevant responses shows that you have been paying attention and understand the speaker's message. Feedback can be as simple as nodding, making affirming sounds such as "uh-huh," or giving a more detailed verbal response. For instance, if a colleague explains a complex problem they are facing, providing constructive feedback like, "That sounds challenging. Have you considered trying a different approach?" can demonstrate your engagement and willingness to help.

Being aware of and managing your own biases and assumptions is critical for active listening. These can cloud your judgment and hinder your ability to truly understand the speaker's perspective. Approach each conversation with an open mind, setting aside preconceived notions and focusing on the speaker's words and feelings. For example, if you disagree with a friend's opinion, rather than immediately countering it, try to understand their reasoning by asking, "What experiences have led you to this viewpoint?" This openness can lead to more productive and respectful dialogues.

Active listening also involves recognizing and responding to the speaker's emotions. This requires paying attention to vocal cues, such as tone, pitch, and pace, which can provide insights into their emotional state. For example, if a colleague's voice sounds tense and hurried, acknowledging their stress by saying, "You seem a bit stressed. How can I support you?" can demonstrate empathy and offer much-needed support. This attention to emotional cues not only deepens your understanding of the speaker's situation but also shows that you care about their well-being.

Asking Powerful Questions

Asking powerful questions is an essential skill that can transform conversations, uncover deeper insights, and foster more meaningful connections. This practice goes beyond simple inquiries; it involves crafting questions that provoke thought, elicit detailed responses, and drive impactful dialogue. Mastering the art of asking powerful questions can enhance your personal and professional interactions, leading to more productive outcomes and enriched relationships.

Consider a situation where you're leading a team meeting to brainstorm solutions for a challenging project. Rather than asking, "Do you have any ideas?" which might yield limited responses, a more powerful question would be, "What innovative approaches can we explore to overcome this specific challenge?" This type of question opens the floor for creativity and encourages team members to think more deeply about potential solutions. It sets the stage for a more dynamic and engaging discussion, where each participant feels invited to contribute their unique perspectives.

One of the key characteristics of powerful questions is that they are open-ended. Open-ended questions cannot be answered with a simple "yes" or "no"; they require the respondent to elaborate, providing richer and more nuanced information. For example, instead of asking a colleague, "Did you like the proposal?" a more powerful question would be, "What aspects of the proposal do you find most compelling, and why?" This not only prompts a more detailed answer but also reveals underlying thoughts and feelings that might not surface with a closed question.

Another hallmark of powerful questions is their ability to encourage reflection and introspection. These questions often begin with "how" or "why," prompting the respondent to explore their motivations, experiences, and thought processes. For instance, if you're mentoring someone and they express uncertainty about their career path, asking, "Why do you feel drawn to this particular field, and how does it align with your long-term goals?" can help them articulate their aspirations and clarify their intentions. This reflective questioning can lead to greater self-awareness and more informed decision-making.

Timing and context are crucial when asking powerful questions. The most effective questions are asked at the right moment, in an appropriate setting, and with a tone that conveys genuine curiosity and respect. For example, during a one-on-one meeting with an employee who seems disengaged, asking, "What factors are affecting your motivation at work, and how can we address them?" shows that you are attuned to their needs and willing to support their well-being. This approach fosters an environment of trust and openness, where the employee feels safe to share their concerns.

Active listening is a vital complement to asking powerful questions. When you pose a deep or probing question, it's essential to listen attentively to the response, demonstrating that you value the speaker's input. This involves maintaining eye contact, nodding in acknowledgment, and refraining from interrupting. For instance, if a team member is explaining their perspective on a project setback, giving them your full attention and responding with follow-up questions like, "Can you elaborate on the challenges you faced?" shows that you are genuinely interested in understanding their experience.

The language you use in your questions can significantly impact the responses you receive. Using positive and empowering language encourages more open and constructive replies. For example, instead of asking, "Why did this project fail?" which might put the respondent on the defensive, you could ask, "What can we learn from the challenges we encountered in this project?" This reframing shifts the focus from blame to growth, fostering a more positive and solution-oriented conversation.

Clarity and specificity are also important when formulating powerful questions. Vague or ambiguous questions can lead to confusion and less effective responses. Being clear about what you want to know helps the respondent understand your intent and provide more relevant information. For instance, rather than asking, "What's going on with the project?" a more specific question would be, "Can you update me on the current status of the project and any obstacles you're encountering?" This specificity helps direct the conversation and ensures you receive the information you need.

Powerful questions can also serve as a tool for conflict resolution. When tensions arise, asking questions that promote understanding and empathy can defuse situations and pave the way for constructive dialogue. For example, if two team members are in disagreement, you might ask, "Can each of you share your perspective on this issue and what you believe is the best way forward?" This invites both parties to voice their viewpoints and fosters a collaborative approach to finding a resolution.

In coaching or mentoring relationships, powerful questions are indispensable for facilitating growth and development. These questions can help individuals identify their strengths, uncover their passions, and set meaningful goals. For example, asking, "What are your key strengths, and how can you leverage them to achieve your career aspirations?" encourages self-reflection and strategic thinking. It helps the mentee gain clarity about their abilities and how they can use them to progress in their career.

In personal relationships, powerful questions can deepen connections and understanding. When engaging in conversations with friends or family, asking questions that explore emotions, values, and experiences can create a stronger bond. For example, instead of the usual "How was your day?" you might ask, "What was the highlight of your day and why?" This type of question encourages the person to reflect on positive experiences and share meaningful moments, fostering a deeper connection between you.

Chapter 3

Nonverbal Communication

Understanding Body Language

Understanding body language is a crucial skill that can significantly enhance your communication abilities. Nonverbal cues often convey more information than spoken words, providing insight into emotions, intentions, and reactions. By learning to interpret these signals accurately, you can improve your interpersonal interactions, build stronger relationships, and navigate social situations more effectively.

Imagine walking into a room where a meeting is already in progress. Before anyone speaks, you can sense the atmosphere. Are people leaning forward, engaged and interested? Or are they slouched back, arms crossed, and faces tense? These observations come from reading body language, which communicates feelings and attitudes that words might not express.

One of the most telling aspects of body language is facial expressions. The human face is incredibly expressive, capable of displaying a wide range of emotions without uttering a single word. Happiness, sadness, anger, surprise, and fear can all be conveyed through subtle changes in facial muscles. For instance, a genuine smile, which involves the crinkling of the eyes as well as the upturning of the mouth, can indicate true happiness or friendliness. On the other hand, a forced smile might lack this eye movement, signaling insincerity or discomfort.

Eye contact is another powerful element of body language. Maintaining appropriate eye contact can convey confidence, interest, and honesty. However, the meaning of eye contact can vary across cultures. In some cultures, direct eye contact is seen as a sign of respect and attentiveness, while in others, it might be considered rude or confrontational. It's important to be aware of these cultural differences to avoid misinterpretation. Generally, consistent but not excessive eye contact is a good practice, balancing engagement without appearing too intense.

Gestures play a significant role in nonverbal communication as well. Hand movements can emphasize points, indicate direction, or express emotions. For example, open palms facing upwards often suggest openness and honesty, while clenched fists may indicate anger or frustration. Pointing can be perceived as aggressive or rude, so it's usually better to use an open hand to indicate something or someone. By being mindful of your gestures, you can reinforce your verbal messages and avoid misunderstandings.

Posture is another critical component of body language. The way you stand or sit can convey a lot about your attitude and confidence. An upright, open posture generally signals confidence and attentiveness, while a slouched or closed posture can indicate disinterest or insecurity. For example, standing with your shoulders back and head held high can make you appear more confident and approachable. In contrast, crossing your arms or legs may be interpreted as defensive or closed off.

Proximity, or personal space, also communicates important nonverbal information. The distance you maintain from others can signal your level of comfort and familiarity. Standing too close to someone can invade their personal space and make them feel uncomfortable, while standing too far away might suggest disengagement or aloofness. The appropriate amount of personal space can vary depending on cultural norms and the nature of the relationship. Being aware of these boundaries can help you interact more comfortably and respectfully with others.

Touch is a powerful, yet often overlooked, aspect of body language. A handshake, pat on the back, or gentle touch on the arm can convey support, agreement, or reassurance. However, the appropriateness of touch depends heavily on the context and the relationship between individuals. In professional settings, a firm handshake can convey confidence and professionalism, while in personal relationships, a hug might express affection and comfort. It's important to be sensitive to others' boundaries and cultural norms regarding touch to avoid discomfort or miscommunication.

Mirroring is a subtle but effective body language technique. It involves subtly mimicking the gestures, posture, and expressions of the person you are interacting with. This can create a sense of rapport and mutual understanding. For example, if someone leans forward while speaking to you, leaning forward slightly can signal that you are engaged and interested. Mirroring can help build a connection and make the other person feel more comfortable and understood.

In addition to reading others' body language, it's crucial to be aware of your nonverbal signals. Self-awareness can help you project the image you want to convey and avoid sending unintended messages. Practicing good posture, maintaining appropriate eye contact, and using gestures thoughtfully can enhance your communication effectiveness. For instance, if you want to appear confident and approachable in a job interview, be mindful of your posture, make eye contact with the interviewer, and use open, positive gestures.

Body language can also play a significant role in conflict resolution. During disagreements, paying attention to nonverbal cues can help you gauge the other person's emotions and adjust your approach accordingly. If you notice signs of frustration or anger, such as crossed arms or a furrowed brow, you might choose to de-escalate the situation by speaking calmly and maintaining an open posture. Similarly, showing empathy through your body language, such as nodding in understanding or leaning slightly forward, can help diffuse tension and promote a more constructive dialogue.

In leadership, effective use of body language can inspire trust and confidence among team members. Leaders who exhibit positive body language can foster a supportive and motivating environment. For example, maintaining an open posture, making eye contact, and using encouraging gestures can make team members feel valued and respected. A leader who nods in agreement, smiles genuinely, and engages physically with the team can create a sense of unity and shared purpose. Conversely, negative body language, such as crossed arms, avoiding eye contact, or distracted behaviors, can undermine authority and erode trust.

The Impact of Facial Expressions

Facial expressions are an integral part of human communication, offering a window into our emotions and thoughts. They are universal, transcending language barriers and cultural differences, and they play a crucial role in how we perceive and interact with one another. Understanding the impact of facial expressions can enhance your ability to connect with others, read their emotions accurately, and convey your own feelings more effectively.

The human face is capable of making over 10,000 different expressions, each conveying a unique combination of emotions. This remarkable range allows us to communicate complex feelings and reactions without uttering a single word. For instance, a smile can indicate happiness, friendliness, or even sarcasm, depending on the context and accompanying expressions. A frown, on the other hand, often signals displeasure, confusion, or concentration. The subtle nuances of these expressions are critical to interpreting the true meaning behind them.

One of the most significant aspects of facial expressions is their ability to convey emotions. Emotions such as joy, sadness, anger, surprise, fear, and disgust are universally recognized through facial expressions. Research has shown that these basic emotions are expressed similarly across different cultures, highlighting the universality of facial expressions. For example, a genuine smile, known as the Duchenne smile, involves the contraction of both the zygomatic major muscle (which raises the corners of the mouth) and the orbicularis oculi muscle (which causes the eyes to crinkle). This type of smile is universally associated with genuine happiness and positive emotions.

Facial expressions also play a crucial role in nonverbal communication, complementing and sometimes even contradicting spoken words. Imagine a scenario where someone says they are fine, but their face tells a different story. Perhaps their lips are pressed tightly together, and their eyebrows are furrowed, indicating tension or discomfort. In such cases, the facial expression provides valuable context that words alone might not convey. This interplay between verbal and nonverbal cues is essential for accurate communication and understanding.

Microexpressions, which are brief, involuntary facial expressions, can reveal true emotions that someone might be trying to conceal. These fleeting expressions, lasting only a fraction of a second, occur when a person attempts to hide their feelings. For instance, a quick flash of anger or sadness might appear on someone's face before they mask it with a neutral expression. Being able to detect and interpret microexpressions can be a powerful tool in understanding others' true emotions, especially in high-stakes situations like negotiations or conflict resolution.

Facial expressions are not only important for understanding others but also for expressing our own emotions and intentions. When we react to situations, our facial expressions can provide immediate feedback to those around us. For example, in a social setting, a look of surprise or delight upon receiving a compliment can reinforce the positive interaction, encouraging further conversation and connection. Conversely, a look of boredom or disinterest can signal to others that the topic or interaction is not engaging, prompting a change in subject or approach.

In professional settings, facial expressions can significantly impact how we are perceived by colleagues, clients, and superiors. A confident, approachable demeanor, characterized by a relaxed face, frequent smiles, and attentive expressions, can foster trust and collaboration. On the other hand, expressions of frustration, anger, or disinterest can create tension and hinder effective communication. Being mindful of your facial expressions in the workplace can help you build better relationships, lead more effectively, and create a positive work environment.

Cultural differences can influence the interpretation of facial expressions, although the basic emotions are universally recognized. For example, in some cultures, direct eye contact and expressive facial gestures are considered important for showing engagement and honesty. In others, such behaviors might be seen as disrespectful or overly aggressive. Understanding these cultural nuances is essential for effective cross-cultural communication. By being aware of and respecting these differences, you can navigate diverse social and professional environments more successfully.

Facial expressions also play a pivotal role in building and maintaining personal relationships. In romantic relationships, for instance, the ability to read and respond to your partner's facial expressions can enhance intimacy and emotional connection. Expressions of love, concern, joy, and even sadness can deepen the bond between partners, fostering a sense of understanding and empathy. Similarly, in friendships, recognizing and responding to a friend's facial cues can strengthen the relationship by showing that you care about their feelings and experiences.

The impact of facial expressions extends to digital communication as well. With the rise of video calls and virtual meetings, facial expressions remain a key component of effective communication. Even in the absence of physical presence, seeing someone's face can provide important emotional context and help build rapport. For instance, a warm smile or a nod of understanding during a video call can create a sense of connection and engagement, making the conversation more effective and satisfying.

Improving your awareness and control of facial expressions can enhance your overall communication skills. Practicing mindfulness and paying attention to your own expressions can help you become more conscious of the messages you are sending. For example, you might notice that you tend to frown or look away when you are deep in thought, which could be misinterpreted as disinterest or disagreement. By becoming aware of these tendencies, you can make more deliberate choices about how to present yourself in different situations.

Gestures and Their Meanings

Gestures are a fundamental aspect of nonverbal communication, playing a crucial role in how we express ourselves and understand others. Unlike words, gestures transcend linguistic barriers and can convey a wealth of information through simple movements of the hands, arms, and body. Understanding the meanings behind various gestures can enhance your ability to communicate effectively in both personal and professional settings.

One of the most common and universally recognized gestures is the wave. A wave can signify a greeting, a farewell, or an attempt to gain someone's attention. The context in which a wave is used significantly influences its interpretation. For example, a small, quick wave with a smile typically signals a friendly greeting, while a more vigorous wave might indicate excitement or urgency. The versatility of this gesture makes it an essential tool in our communication repertoire.

Handshakes are another widely recognized gesture, particularly in professional environments. They can convey respect, agreement, and the initiation or conclusion of a social or business interaction. The firmness of a handshake often communicates different messages: a firm grip can indicate confidence and assertiveness, while a limp handshake might be perceived as a lack of enthusiasm or confidence. Cultural differences also play a role in how handshakes are perceived; for instance, in some cultures, a long handshake is a sign of respect, while in others, a brief handshake is more customary.

Thumbs-up is a gesture that generally conveys approval or agreement. Its meaning is widely understood in many parts of the world, making it a convenient and effective way to express positive feedback or affirmation. However, it's important to be aware of cultural variations; in some countries, the thumbs-up gesture may have different or even negative connotations. For example, in parts of the Middle East, a thumbs-up can be considered rude or offensive. Being mindful of such cultural differences is essential to avoid misunderstandings.

Pointing with the index finger is a gesture commonly used to direct attention or indicate a specific object or person. While it can be a practical way to guide someone's focus, pointing can also be perceived as rude or aggressive in certain cultures. In many Asian cultures, for instance, pointing directly at someone is considered impolite. Instead, people use their entire hand or chin to indicate direction. Understanding these cultural nuances can help you navigate social interactions more gracefully.

The OK sign, made by forming a circle with the thumb and index finger, is another gesture with varied interpretations. In many Western countries, it signifies that everything is fine or satisfactory. However, this gesture can have negative meanings in other parts of the world. In Brazil, for instance, it is considered vulgar and offensive. In some parts of Europe, it can imply worthlessness or zero. Such differences highlight the importance of cultural awareness in interpreting and using gestures appropriately.

Nodding and shaking the head are gestures universally associated with agreement and disagreement, respectively. Nodding typically signals affirmation or understanding, while shaking the head indicates negation or disapproval. These gestures are straightforward and widely recognized, making them effective tools for nonverbal communication. However, in certain cultures, such as in parts of Bulgaria and Greece, these gestures can have opposite meanings, with a nod meaning "no" and a shake meaning "yes." Being aware of these exceptions is crucial for accurate communication.

Crossed arms are often interpreted as a defensive or closed-off gesture. When someone crosses their arms during a conversation, it might indicate that they are feeling uncomfortable, resistant, or defensive. However, context matters; sometimes crossed arms can simply mean that a person is cold or seeking comfort. Paying attention to accompanying facial expressions and body language can provide additional clues to the true meaning behind this gesture.

Open palm gestures, such as spreading the hands with palms facing up, generally convey openness, honesty, and a willingness to communicate. This gesture is often used in speeches and presentations to engage the audience and emphasize sincerity. In contrast, a closed fist or clenched hands can signal anger, frustration, or determination. Recognizing these subtle differences can help you better understand the emotions and intentions behind someone's gestures.

Gestures also play a significant role in signaling emotions. For example, a clenched fist can signify anger or determination, while rubbing the forehead might indicate stress or deep thought. Tapping fingers or feet can suggest impatience or anxiety. These small, often subconscious movements provide valuable insights into a person's emotional state, helping you respond more empathetically in social interactions.

In professional settings, gestures can enhance your ability to communicate effectively and build rapport. During presentations, using purposeful gestures can help emphasize key points and engage the audience. For instance, pointing upwards can signify importance or aspiration, while spreading your hands apart can indicate inclusivity or a broad concept. Being mindful of your gestures can make your communication more dynamic and impactful.

Gestures also play a pivotal role in negotiations and conflict resolution. Open gestures, such as uncrossed arms and visible palms, can help create a sense of trust and openness, facilitating more productive discussions. Conversely, closed or aggressive gestures, such as pointing or clenched fists, can escalate tensions and hinder resolution. Being aware of your gestures and those of others can significantly impact the outcome of a negotiation or conflict. By consciously adopting open and inviting gestures, you can foster a more collaborative atmosphere, encouraging mutual understanding and agreement.

The Role of Eye Contact

Eye contact is one of the most powerful forms of nonverbal communication, profoundly influencing the dynamics of interpersonal interactions. Whether in personal conversations, professional settings, or public speaking, the ability to effectively use and interpret eye contact can significantly enhance communication, build trust, and convey a wide range of emotions and intentions.

In personal interactions, eye contact serves as a fundamental component of connection and empathy. When two people maintain eye contact, it creates a sense of intimacy and mutual understanding. For instance, during a heartfelt conversation with a friend, sustained eye contact can convey genuine interest and concern, making the other person feel heard and valued. Conversely, avoiding eye contact can suggest discomfort, disinterest, or even deceit. This is why maintaining appropriate eye contact is crucial for fostering trust and openness in relationships.

In professional environments, eye contact plays a pivotal role in establishing authority, confidence, and engagement. During meetings or presentations, making eye contact with colleagues and audience members can help assert your presence and command attention. A speaker who maintains eye contact with their audience is more likely to be perceived as confident and credible, thereby enhancing the effectiveness of their message. On the other hand, avoiding eye contact can undermine your authority and make you appear uncertain or untrustworthy.

The nuances of eye contact vary across different cultures, and being aware of these differences is essential for effective cross-cultural communication. In some cultures, direct eye contact is seen as a sign of honesty and confidence, while in others, it may be considered disrespectful or confrontational. For example, in many Western cultures, maintaining eye contact is encouraged and seen as a sign of attentiveness and respect. In contrast, in some Asian cultures, prolonged eye contact may be perceived as rude or aggressive. Understanding these cultural variations can help you navigate international interactions more sensitively and avoid potential misunderstandings.

Eye contact is also a critical tool in active listening. When engaged in a conversation, maintaining eye contact shows the speaker that you are fully present and attentive. It signals that you value their words and are interested in what they have to say. This can foster a more open and productive dialogue, as the speaker feels encouraged to share their thoughts and feelings. Additionally, by observing the speaker's eye contact and facial expressions, you can gain deeper insights into their emotions and intentions, allowing for a more empathetic and nuanced response.

In the realm of public speaking, eye contact can significantly impact the effectiveness of your delivery. Engaging with your audience through eye contact can help establish a connection, making your speech more compelling and relatable. By scanning the room and making eye contact with different individuals, you can create a sense of inclusivity and keep the audience engaged. This technique helps to break down barriers and makes the audience feel as though you are speaking directly to them, enhancing the overall impact of your message.

Eye contact also plays a crucial role in nonverbal cues that complement verbal communication. For instance, a fleeting glance or a prolonged stare can convey a wealth of information that words alone might not fully capture. A brief, furtive look can suggest hesitation or doubt, while steady eye contact can indicate confidence and assurance. These subtle cues can enhance or alter the meaning of spoken words, adding depth and complexity to the interaction.

In romantic relationships, eye contact can deepen emotional bonds and enhance intimacy. Gazing into a partner's eyes can create a powerful sense of connection and mutual understanding. This form of eye contact can communicate love, desire, and affection in ways that words often cannot. It is a silent yet potent form of expression that can strengthen the emotional fabric of a relationship.

Children also rely heavily on eye contact as part of their developmental process. From an early age, infants seek eye contact with their caregivers to form secure attachments and communicate their needs. As children grow, eye contact continues to play a vital role in their social and emotional development. It helps them learn to interpret social cues, understand emotions, and develop empathy. Encouraging children to maintain eye contact during conversations can support their interpersonal skills and confidence.

In virtual communication, where physical presence is limited, eye contact remains an important element. Although direct eye contact is not possible through screens, looking into the camera can simulate eye contact, creating a sense of connection and engagement. This is particularly important in remote work environments, where building rapport and maintaining effective communication are crucial. By being mindful of your virtual eye contact, you can enhance the quality of your online interactions and foster stronger relationships with colleagues and clients.

The role of eye contact in conflict resolution cannot be overstated. During disagreements or difficult conversations, maintaining eye contact can demonstrate that you are willing to engage openly and honestly. It signals that you are committed to resolving the issue and are not avoiding the confrontation. This can help de-escalate tensions and facilitate a more constructive dialogue. However, it is important to balance assertiveness with empathy, as overly intense eye contact can be perceived as aggressive or intimidating.

In summary, eye contact is a multifaceted and powerful tool in human communication. It serves as a bridge between individuals, conveying emotions, intentions, and levels of engagement without the need for words. Mastering the use of eye contact can significantly enhance your interpersonal skills and improve the quality of your interactions in various contexts.

Personal Space and Proxemics

Navigating the subtle nuances of personal space and proxemics is an essential skill that can significantly impact the success of social, professional, and intimate interactions. Personal space refers to the physical distance we maintain between ourselves and others, while proxemics is the study of how we use space in communication and social interactions. Understanding and respecting these spatial boundaries is crucial for building healthy and respectful relationships.

Personal space varies widely depending on cultural norms, individual preferences, and the nature of the relationship between the people involved. In general, there are four zones of personal space: intimate, personal, social, and public. Intimate space is typically reserved for close family members, partners, and very close friends, encompassing a distance of up to 18 inches. This zone is where our most private and vulnerable interactions occur, such as hugging, whispering, or comforting someone in distress.

Personal space extends from 18 inches to about 4 feet and is the distance we maintain with friends and acquaintances. This zone allows for comfortable interactions while still providing a sense of personal autonomy. For example, when catching up with a friend over coffee, you might sit within this personal space range, fostering a sense of closeness without invading each other's comfort zones.

Social space ranges from 4 to 12 feet and is typically used in professional or casual social settings, such as business meetings or social gatherings. This distance allows for clear communication while maintaining a level of formality and respect. In a meeting with colleagues, for instance, you would likely position yourself within this social space to engage in discussion without encroaching on their personal space.

Public space, extending beyond 12 feet, is the distance we maintain in public speaking or when interacting with larger groups. This zone is characterized by a sense of detachment and formality, as it is used for addressing audiences or large gatherings. A speaker at a conference, for example, would use public space to engage with the audience while maintaining a clear physical boundary.

Cultural differences play a significant role in determining acceptable distances for personal space. In some cultures, close physical proximity is a sign of warmth and friendliness, while in others, it may be perceived as intrusive or disrespectful. For instance, people from Mediterranean and Latin American cultures often stand closer to one another during conversations compared to those from Northern European or East Asian cultures, where more personal space is typically preferred. Being aware of these cultural variations can help you navigate cross-cultural interactions more effectively and avoid potential misunderstandings.

Proxemics also encompasses the use of body language and physical positioning in communication. The way we orient our bodies, the direction of our gaze, and our postures all convey important nonverbal messages. For example, facing someone directly and leaning slightly forward can signal interest and engagement, while turning your body away or crossing your arms might indicate discomfort or disinterest. Understanding these nonverbal cues can enhance your ability to interpret and respond to others' needs and emotions appropriately.

In professional settings, proxemics can influence the dynamics of power and authority. The physical arrangement of a room, the positioning of furniture, and the distance between individuals can all impact the perceived hierarchy and level of formality. For example, in a business meeting, the person sitting at the head of the table is often viewed as the leader or authority figure. Similarly, maintaining a certain distance when speaking with superiors can convey respect and professionalism. Being mindful of these spatial dynamics can help you navigate professional environments more effectively and establish positive working relationships.

In personal relationships, respecting personal space is crucial for maintaining trust and intimacy. Invading someone's personal space without consent can lead to discomfort and tension, potentially harming the relationship. For instance, if a friend consistently stands too close for comfort, it may cause you to feel uneasy and less willing to engage with them. On the other hand, respecting personal space and being attuned to nonverbal cues can foster a sense of safety and mutual respect, enhancing the quality of your interactions.

In romantic relationships, the negotiation of personal space can be particularly nuanced. Partners often develop a unique spatial dynamic that balances intimacy with individual autonomy. While closeness and physical affection are important for building emotional bonds, it is equally important to respect each other's need for personal space and independence. This balance can vary greatly from one couple to another and may change over time as the relationship evolves. Open communication about personal space preferences can help partners navigate these dynamics and strengthen their connection.

Personal space and proxemics are also critical in conflict resolution. During heated discussions or disagreements, maintaining an appropriate distance can help de-escalate tensions and create a more conducive environment for constructive dialogue. Standing too close during a conflict can be perceived as aggressive or confrontational, potentially exacerbating the situation. Conversely, maintaining a respectful distance can signal a willingness to listen and engage in a calm and rational manner. This approach can facilitate more effective communication and increase the likelihood of resolving the conflict amicably.

In social gatherings, being mindful of personal space can enhance your social interactions and make others feel more comfortable. For example, when mingling at a party, being conscious of how close you stand to others can help create an inviting and respectful atmosphere. If you notice someone stepping back or turning their body away, it might be a sign that they need more space. Adapting your position accordingly shows sensitivity to their comfort and can make your interactions more positive.

Using Nonverbal Cues to Enhance Your Message

Nonverbal communication is a powerful tool that can significantly enhance the effectiveness of your message. While words are essential for conveying information, nonverbal cues—such as facial expressions, gestures, posture, and eye contact—often speak louder than words. These cues can reinforce your message, convey emotions, and build rapport with your audience. Mastering the art of nonverbal communication can transform how you interact with others, whether in personal relationships, professional settings, or public speaking engagements.

Body language is one of the most critical components of nonverbal communication. Your posture, gestures, and movements can convey confidence, openness, and engagement or, conversely, nervousness, defensiveness, and disengagement. For instance, standing tall with your shoulders back and maintaining an open stance can project confidence and authority. In contrast, slouching or crossing your arms might signal insecurity or defensiveness. Being mindful of your body language and making conscious adjustments can help you present yourself more effectively and positively.

Facial expressions are another vital aspect of nonverbal communication. They can convey a wide range of emotions, from happiness and surprise to anger and sadness. Smiling, for example, can create a sense of warmth and approachability, making others more likely to engage with you. Conversely, frowning or displaying a stern expression can create a barrier and make interactions more challenging. It is essential to be aware of your facial expressions and ensure they align with the message you want to convey. Practicing in front of a mirror or seeking feedback from others can help you refine your expressions and use them more effectively.

Eye contact is a powerful nonverbal cue that can significantly impact communication. It can convey confidence, interest, and sincerity, helping to build trust and rapport. Maintaining appropriate eye contact shows that you are engaged and attentive, making the other person feel valued and understood. However, it's important to strike a balance; too much eye contact can be perceived as intense or aggressive, while too little can seem evasive or disinterested. Practicing good eye contact involves looking at the other person for a few seconds at a time, then briefly glancing away before re-engaging. This approach can help you maintain a natural and comfortable level of eye contact.

Gestures are an integral part of nonverbal communication and can enhance the clarity and impact of your message. Hand movements, for example, can emphasize key points and help illustrate your ideas. Open and expansive gestures can convey enthusiasm and confidence, while closed or minimal gestures might indicate hesitation or discomfort. However, it's important to use gestures purposefully and avoid overdoing them, as excessive or erratic movements can be distracting. Observing skilled speakers and practicing your gestures can help you use them more effectively to reinforce your message.

Proxemics, or the use of personal space, also plays a crucial role in nonverbal communication. The physical distance you maintain from others can convey various messages about your relationship and comfort level. Standing too close might be perceived as intrusive, while standing too far away could signal disinterest or detachment. Being aware of personal space preferences and adjusting your distance accordingly can help create a more comfortable and respectful interaction. In professional settings, maintaining an appropriate distance can also convey professionalism and respect.

Touch is another powerful nonverbal cue that can communicate empathy, support, and connection. A handshake, pat on the back, or light touch on the arm can convey warmth and solidarity. However, the appropriateness of touch varies widely across cultures and individual preferences, so it's essential to be mindful of these differences and seek consent when necessary. In professional settings, touch should generally be limited to formal gestures like handshakes to maintain appropriate boundaries.

Paralanguage, which includes vocal elements such as tone, pitch, volume, and rate of speech, is another crucial aspect of nonverbal communication. The way you say something can often be more important than the words themselves. A warm, enthusiastic tone can convey excitement and positivity, while a monotone or flat voice might indicate boredom or disinterest. Similarly, speaking too quickly can make it difficult for others to follow your message, while speaking too slowly might cause them to lose interest. Practicing vocal variety and paying attention to how you use your voice can enhance the effectiveness of your communication.

Nonverbal cues also play a significant role in active listening. Demonstrating that you are fully engaged in the conversation through nodding, maintaining eye contact, and using affirming gestures can make the other person feel heard and valued. Mirroring the other person's body language can also help build rapport and create a sense of connection. Active listening involves not only hearing the words but also understanding the emotions and intentions behind them, which can be conveyed through nonverbal cues.

Cultural differences in nonverbal communication are essential to consider, as they can affect how your message is received and interpreted. Gestures, personal space, touch, and eye contact norms can vary significantly across cultures. For example, in some cultures, maintaining direct eye contact is a sign of confidence and respect, while in others, it might be considered disrespectful or confrontational. Similarly, while a firm handshake is a common greeting in many Western cultures, in some Asian cultures, a bow might be more appropriate. Being aware of these cultural variations and adjusting your nonverbal communication accordingly can help you avoid misunderstandings and build more effective cross-cultural relationships.

Chapter 4

Building Trust Through Communication

The Importance of Trust in Relationships

Trust is the cornerstone of any meaningful relationship. Whether it's a bond between friends, family members, romantic partners, or colleagues, trust forms the foundation upon which these connections are built. Without trust, relationships can crumble under the weight of doubt, suspicion, and insecurity. Understanding the importance of trust and how to cultivate it can lead to stronger, more resilient connections with the people in your life.

Consider the story of Jane and Mark, a married couple who have been together for over a decade. Early in their relationship, they faced numerous challenges, including financial stress and demanding careers. Despite these pressures, they managed to maintain a strong bond, largely because they trusted each other implicitly. Jane knew that she could rely on Mark to support her decisions, and Mark felt confident that Jane would always have his back. This mutual trust allowed them to navigate their difficulties with a united front, ultimately strengthening their marriage.

Trust is built through consistent actions over time. It's about showing up for the people you care about, being reliable, and demonstrating integrity. For example, if a friend confides in you and asks you to keep their secret, honoring that request builds trust. Conversely, breaking that confidence can cause irreparable damage to the relationship. It's the accumulation of these small, trust-building actions that reinforce the reliability and dependability essential to any strong bond.

Reliability is a critical component of trust. When you make a promise or commit to something, following through is vital. Imagine you promised a colleague that you'd help them with a project by a specific deadline. If you deliver on time, you reinforce their trust in your reliability. If you fail to meet the deadline without a valid reason, you risk damaging that trust. Being reliable means others can count on you to do what you say you will do, which is integral to maintaining trust.

Honesty is another key element in establishing trust. This doesn't mean brutal honesty that disregards feelings, but rather a commitment to truthfulness and transparency. If you make a mistake, owning up to it rather than covering it up can actually build trust. People appreciate honesty, even when the truth is difficult to hear. It shows that you respect them enough to be forthright. On the other hand, dishonesty erodes trust and can lead to a breakdown in communication and connection.

Empathy plays a significant role in fostering trust. When others feel that you genuinely understand and care about their experiences and emotions, they're more likely to trust you. Empathy involves active listening and responding with compassion. For instance, if a friend is going through a tough time, simply being there to listen and offer support can deepen their trust in you. It's about showing that you value their feelings and are willing to be there for them, no matter what.

Building trust also requires vulnerability. Sharing your own thoughts, feelings, and experiences can encourage others to open up as well. Vulnerability fosters intimacy and connection, as it shows that you trust the other person enough to reveal your authentic self. This can be particularly powerful in romantic relationships, where mutual vulnerability can lead to a deeper emotional bond.

Consistency is crucial in maintaining trust. It's not enough to be trustworthy in a few isolated instances; it requires a sustained effort over time. If you're consistently honest, reliable, and empathetic, you build a solid foundation of trust that can withstand challenges. Inconsistent behavior, on the other hand, can create uncertainty and doubt, undermining the trust you've worked hard to build.

Trust is not static; it evolves and can be strengthened or weakened over time. Life's ups and downs will test the trust in any relationship. During difficult times, trust can be a stabilizing force that helps you navigate challenges together. For example, if a family faces financial hardship, the trust between its members can provide the emotional support needed to get through tough times. Knowing that you can rely on each other can make a significant difference in overcoming adversity.

Repairing broken trust is challenging but possible. It requires a genuine commitment to change, transparency, and patience. If you've breached someone's trust, acknowledging the hurt you've caused and demonstrating through consistent actions that you're committed to rebuilding that trust is essential. It's a gradual process and cannot be rushed. The person whose trust was broken needs time to heal and decide if they're willing to trust again.

Forgiveness is a critical component in the process of rebuilding trust. Holding onto grudges can prevent relationships from moving forward. While forgiving someone who has broken your trust is difficult, it's a necessary step towards healing. Forgiveness doesn't mean forgetting or excusing the behavior, but rather letting go of the resentment and working towards rebuilding the relationship.

Trust also plays a vital role in professional settings. In the workplace, trust between colleagues can lead to more effective collaboration, increased productivity, and a more positive work environment. When team members trust each other, they're more likely to share ideas, take risks, and support one another. This can lead to innovative solutions and a stronger, more cohesive team.

Leadership and trust are inextricably linked. Effective leaders understand that earning the trust of their team is paramount. They do this by demonstrating integrity, competence, and empathy. A leader who communicates transparently, follows through on commitments, and shows genuine concern for their team members' well-being fosters a culture of trust.

This, in turn, can lead to increased employee engagement, loyalty, and overall job satisfaction.

Communicating with Integrity

Imagine a world where every word spoken is true, every promise made is kept, and every conversation is conducted with genuine respect and honesty. This ideal may seem unattainable, but it serves as a guiding star for anyone striving to communicate with integrity. Integrity in communication is not just about avoiding lies; it's about aligning your words and actions with your values, showing respect for others, and fostering trust. By committing to integrity, you can transform your interactions and build stronger, more meaningful relationships.

Consider the story of Maria, a manager at a mid-sized technology company. Maria was known for her clear, honest communication style. When her team faced a challenging project with tight deadlines, she didn't sugarcoat the difficulties. Instead, she openly discussed the hurdles, acknowledged the team's concerns, and laid out a realistic plan. Her transparency did more than just build trust; it empowered her team to tackle the project with a clear understanding of the stakes and their roles. Maria's commitment to integrity in communication created an environment where her team felt respected and valued, ultimately leading to their success.

One of the fundamental aspects of communicating with integrity is honesty. This doesn't mean you need to disclose everything to everyone, but it does mean being truthful and straightforward in your interactions. Honesty helps avoid misunderstandings and builds a foundation of trust. For example, if you make a mistake at work, admitting it promptly and taking responsibility can prevent further complications and demonstrate your reliability. This kind of honesty shows your commitment to ethical behavior and respect for those around you.

However, honesty should be balanced with tact. Being honest doesn't require harshness. Delivering difficult truths with empathy can preserve relationships and show that you care about the other person's feelings. If you need to give negative feedback, focus on the behavior rather than the person, and offer constructive suggestions for improvement. This approach not only maintains integrity but also fosters a positive and supportive environment.

Another key component of integrity in communication is consistency. Your words and actions should align, and you should convey the same message across different contexts. If you tell your team that you value punctuality, but you frequently arrive late to meetings, your inconsistency undermines your message and erodes trust. Consistency demonstrates that you stand by your principles and can be relied upon to follow through on your commitments.

Active listening is also crucial for communicating with integrity. It involves fully engaging with the speaker, understanding their message, and responding thoughtfully. This practice shows respect for the other person and ensures that communication is a two-way street. When you listen actively, you validate the speaker's perspective and demonstrate that you value their input. This can deepen mutual respect and strengthen your relationship.

Consider the case of John, who worked in a customer service role. John was known for his exceptional listening skills. When customers called in with complaints, he didn't just hear their words; he listened to their frustrations and empathized with their experiences. By acknowledging their feelings and working diligently to resolve their issues, John consistently communicated with integrity. His approach not only resolved conflicts but also turned dissatisfied customers into loyal advocates for the company.

Transparency is another important aspect of integrity in communication. Being open about your intentions, decisions, and processes can prevent misunderstandings and build trust. However, transparency should be balanced with discretion. It's important to share information that is relevant and appropriate for the situation, while respecting confidentiality when necessary. For instance, a leader might transparently explain the reasons behind a significant organizational change, while withholding sensitive details that could harm the company or its employees if disclosed.

Communicating with integrity also involves being accountable. When you make a commitment, follow through and meet your obligations. If circumstances change and you can't fulfill a promise, communicate this promptly and honestly. Taking responsibility for your actions, especially when things go wrong, shows that you are dependable and trustworthy. Accountability reinforces the trust others place in you and demonstrates your commitment to ethical behavior.

Empathy is integral to communication with integrity. Understanding and acknowledging others' feelings fosters a supportive and respectful environment. Empathy involves more than just listening; it requires you to put yourself in the other person's shoes and respond with compassion. For instance, if a colleague is going through a tough time, expressing your understanding and offering support can strengthen your relationship and demonstrate your integrity.

Integrity in communication also means avoiding gossip and negative talk about others. Speaking ill of others behind their backs not only harms your credibility but also creates a toxic environment. Instead, aim to speak positively and constructively. If you have an issue with someone, address it directly and respectfully with them. This approach shows that you are committed to honesty and respect, even in difficult situations.

Consider the example of Lisa, who worked in a busy office environment. Despite the prevalent culture of gossip, Lisa chose to abstain from negative conversations about colleagues. When approached with gossip, she would steer the conversation towards more constructive topics or simply excuse herself. Her behavior earned her the respect of her peers and set a positive example for others. By refusing to engage in gossip, Lisa communicated with integrity and fostered a more respectful workplace culture.

Communicating with integrity also involves clarity. Clear communication ensures that your message is understood and reduces the risk of misinterpretation. This means being precise with your language, avoiding jargon when unnecessary, and ensuring that your message aligns with your intended meaning. For example, when assigning tasks to your team, providing clear instructions and setting explicit expectations can prevent confusion and ensure that everyone is on the same page.

Transparency and Openness

Transparency and openness are foundational pillars of any thriving organization or relationship. When individuals and leaders embrace these principles, they foster an environment of trust, accountability, and collaboration. Imagine an organization where information flows freely, decisions are made with clarity, and everyone feels included and valued. This is the vision that transparency and openness aim to achieve.

Consider the story of Alex, a newly appointed CEO of a mid-sized company facing declining morale and productivity. Alex quickly realized that the root of the problem was a lack of transparency. The previous management had kept employees in the dark about the company's financial struggles and strategic decisions, leading to a pervasive sense of uncertainty and mistrust. Determined to turn things around, Alex implemented a policy of radical transparency. He began holding weekly all-hands meetings where he shared detailed updates on the company's performance, challenges, and goals. Employees were encouraged to ask questions and voice their concerns openly. This shift not only improved morale but also sparked a wave of innovative ideas and solutions from employees who felt more invested in the company's success.

Transparency starts with clear and open communication. This involves sharing relevant information promptly and ensuring that everyone has access to the data they need to perform their roles effectively. For instance, in a project team, transparency might mean regularly updating all members on the project's progress, challenges, and any changes in scope or deadlines. This practice helps prevent misunderstandings and ensures that everyone is aligned towards the same goals.

However, transparency is not just about sharing information; it's also about how that information is shared. Clarity is crucial. When communicating complex information, it's important to break it down into understandable chunks and avoid jargon that might confuse or alienate the audience. This approach not only makes the information more accessible but also demonstrates respect for the recipients' ability to understand and engage with the content.

Openness, on the other hand, involves fostering an environment where people feel safe to express their thoughts, ideas, and concerns without fear of judgment or retribution. This can be particularly challenging in hierarchical organizations where power dynamics often discourage open dialogue. Leaders can promote openness by actively seeking input from all levels of the organization, showing genuine interest in employees' perspectives, and responding constructively to feedback.

Consider the example of Julia, a team leader in a large corporation. Julia noticed that her team was hesitant to share their ideas during meetings. To address this, she introduced a practice of anonymous idea submissions before each meeting. This allowed team members to contribute their thoughts without the fear of being judged. Over time, as trust grew, more employees felt comfortable speaking up openly. Julia's commitment to openness not only led to a more engaged and innovative team but also improved the overall team dynamics and performance.

Transparency and openness also play a critical role in decision-making processes. When leaders make decisions behind closed doors, it can lead to confusion, mistrust, and a lack of buy-in from those affected by the decisions. By involving team members in the decision-making process and clearly explaining the rationale behind decisions, leaders can foster a sense of ownership and commitment. This doesn't mean that every decision needs to be made democratically, but providing transparency about the decision-making process and considering input from various stakeholders can lead to better outcomes.

For instance, when a company needs to implement significant changes, such as restructuring or layoffs, transparency is essential. Employees should be informed about the reasons behind the changes, the criteria used for decision-making, and the expected impact. This approach can help mitigate the anxiety and uncertainty that often accompany such changes and demonstrate respect for the employees' right to understand what is happening and why.

Openness also involves being receptive to feedback and willing to make adjustments based on that feedback. This requires a culture where feedback is seen not as criticism but as a valuable tool for improvement. Leaders can model this behavior by actively seeking feedback on their performance and showing a willingness to change based on that feedback. This not only sets a powerful example but also encourages others to embrace a similar mindset.

Consider the case of Mark, a manager who struggled with high turnover in his department. Mark decided to conduct exit interviews with departing employees to understand their reasons for leaving. He discovered that many felt their contributions were not valued and that there was a lack of career development opportunities. Armed with this feedback, Mark made a concerted effort to recognize employees' achievements and implement career development programs. Over time, these changes led to increased employee satisfaction and reduced turnover. Mark's openness to feedback and willingness to act on it demonstrated his commitment to creating a better work environment.

While transparency and openness are generally positive, they must be balanced with discretion. Not all information can or should be shared openly, especially when it involves sensitive matters such as personal data, legal issues, or confidential business strategies. Leaders need to exercise judgment in determining what information to share and how to share it, ensuring that transparency does not compromise privacy or security.

Additionally, transparency and openness require consistency. Sporadic transparency can be perceived as manipulative or insincere. For these principles to be effective, they need to be ingrained in the organization's culture and practiced consistently over time. This means that transparency and openness are not just occasional gestures but integral parts of how the organization operates daily. For example, during regular team meetings, leaders should consistently update the team on relevant developments, share progress towards goals, and transparently discuss any challenges the team is facing. This routine practice helps to normalize transparency and openness, making them part of the organizational DNA.

Building Rapport Quickly

Building rapport quickly is an essential skill in both personal and professional settings. Whether you're meeting a new colleague, initiating a business deal, or simply trying to connect with someone at a social event, the ability to establish a strong, positive connection can significantly impact the outcome of these interactions. This chapter delves into practical strategies and techniques to build rapport effectively and swiftly.

Imagine walking into a room full of strangers at a networking event. The air is thick with the hum of conversations, and you feel a bit out of place. Your goal is to make meaningful connections, but how do you start? The first step is to approach with a genuine smile and open body language. Your non-verbal cues play a crucial role in how others perceive you. A warm smile, eye contact, and a relaxed posture can signal that you are approachable and friendly, setting the stage for a positive interaction.

Once you've made initial contact, the next step is to find common ground. Shared interests or experiences can serve as a bridge between two people. For instance, if you're at a conference, discussing the keynote speaker or a recent session can be an excellent icebreaker. Ask open-ended questions that encourage the other person to share more about themselves. Questions like, "What brought you to this event?" or "What do you enjoy most about your work?" can open up the conversation and reveal commonalities.

Active listening is another vital component of building rapport. This goes beyond just hearing the words the other person is saying; it involves fully engaging with their message. Nodding in agreement, maintaining eye contact, and providing verbal affirmations like "I see" or "That's interesting" can show that you are genuinely interested in what they have to say. Reflecting back what you've heard, such as "So, you've been working on this project for six months?" can also demonstrate that you are paying attention and value their input.

Personal anecdotes and appropriate self-disclosure can help deepen the connection. Sharing a bit about yourself can make you more relatable and human. However, it's essential to strike a balance. Oversharing too soon can be off-putting, while sharing too little can make you seem distant. Aim to disclose information that is relevant to the conversation and mirrors the level of personal information shared by the other person.

Empathy is another powerful tool in building rapport. Showing that you understand and appreciate the other person's feelings and perspectives can create a strong emotional connection. Simple statements like, "I can see why that would be challenging" or "That sounds like a fantastic opportunity" can validate their experiences and foster a sense of mutual understanding.

Remember the importance of names. Dale Carnegie famously said, "A person's name is, to that person, the sweetest sound in any language." Using someone's name in conversation can make the interaction more personal and attentive. If you're bad with names, try associating their name with something familiar or repeating it several times during the conversation to help it stick.

Mirroring is a subtle yet effective technique to build rapport quickly. This involves mimicking the other person's body language, speech patterns, and tone of voice. If they are speaking softly and slowly, try to match their pace and volume. Mirroring can create a subconscious sense of familiarity and comfort, making the other person feel more at ease. However, it's crucial to be subtle and natural in your approach to avoid coming off as insincere or mocking.

Finding opportunities to give genuine compliments can also enhance rapport. People appreciate being recognized for their efforts and achievements. Compliments should be specific and sincere, focusing on something you genuinely admire about the person. For example, "I really admire your dedication to this project" or "Your insights during the meeting were very thought-provoking" can go a long way in building a positive connection.

Humor can be a powerful rapport-building tool when used appropriately. Sharing a light-hearted joke or funny anecdote can break the ice and create a relaxed atmosphere. However, it's important to gauge the other person's sense of humor and avoid jokes that could be offensive or inappropriate. A good rule of thumb is to keep humor light and inclusive.

In professional settings, demonstrating competence and reliability can also build rapport. People are more likely to trust and connect with those they perceive as capable and dependable. Follow through on your commitments, be punctual, and show respect for the other person's time and efforts. Reliability builds a foundation of trust, which is essential for long-term rapport.

Cultural awareness is another crucial aspect of building rapport, especially in diverse environments. Understanding and respecting cultural differences can prevent misunderstandings and foster mutual respect. This might involve learning about different communication styles, social norms, and etiquette practices. For example, in some cultures, direct eye contact may be seen as confrontational, while in others, it is a sign of confidence and honesty. Being mindful of these differences can help you navigate cross-cultural interactions more effectively.

Feedback is a valuable tool for maintaining and deepening rapport over time. Asking for feedback on your interactions shows that you value the other person's perspective and are committed to improving your relationship.

When you receive feedback, listen attentively and respond constructively. This demonstrates that you respect their opinions and are willing to make adjustments. For instance, if a colleague mentions that they prefer more detailed updates during project meetings, acknowledge their preference and make an effort to provide the information they need in future meetings.

Maintaining Trust Over Time

Trust is the cornerstone of any meaningful relationship, whether personal or professional. Building trust is one thing, but maintaining it over time requires consistent effort, transparency, and a genuine commitment to integrity. Trust is not a one-time achievement; it's an ongoing process that can be fragile and requires nurturing. This chapter delves into the strategies and practices needed to maintain trust over time, ensuring that relationships remain strong and resilient.

Consider the story of Robert, a project manager at a mid-sized tech company. When Robert first joined the team, he quickly gained the trust of his colleagues by delivering on his promises and being transparent about project timelines and challenges. However, as projects became more complex and the team expanded, maintaining that initial trust required more than just punctuality and honesty—it required a deeper level of engagement and consistency.

One of the foundational practices for maintaining trust is consistent communication. Regular updates, whether through meetings, emails, or informal check-ins, keep everyone informed and aligned. When people feel that they are kept in the loop, their trust in the leader grows. Robert, for instance, implemented weekly team meetings where he not only shared progress but also openly discussed any setbacks. This transparency reassured the team that he was not hiding anything and was committed to navigating challenges together.

Accountability is another crucial element in maintaining trust. This means taking responsibility for your actions and their outcomes, whether good or bad. When mistakes happen, acknowledging them promptly and taking corrective action demonstrates integrity. Robert made it a point to own up to any errors on his part, whether it was a miscalculation in a timeline or a communication lapse. This willingness to accept responsibility and learn from mistakes reinforced his team's trust in him.

Reliability is equally important. Consistently meeting deadlines, following through on commitments, and being dependable in your role show others that they can count on you. Reliability builds a track record of trustworthiness. Robert's team knew they could rely on him because he consistently delivered what he promised. This reliability was not just about meeting deadlines but also about being present and available when the team needed support.

Empathy plays a significant role in maintaining trust. Understanding and valuing the perspectives and feelings of others foster a deeper connection. When team members feel heard and understood, their trust in their leader strengthens. Robert made it a priority to listen to his team's concerns and feedback actively. He encouraged open dialogue and made adjustments based on their input, showing that he valued their contributions and well-being.

Transparency in decision-making is another key practice. When leaders are open about the reasons behind their decisions, it builds trust. People feel more secure when they understand the "why" behind actions that affect them. Robert ensured transparency by explaining the rationale behind project changes or new initiatives. This openness helped the team feel involved and respected, even when decisions were tough or unpopular.

Building trust also involves respecting confidentiality. In any relationship, there will be sensitive information that must be handled with discretion. Maintaining confidentiality shows that you can be trusted with important matters, fostering a safe environment for open communication. Robert was careful to keep private any personal or sensitive information shared with him by team members, further solidifying their trust in him.

Consistency between words and actions is critical. When people's actions align with their words, it reinforces their credibility. Conversely, saying one thing and doing another can quickly erode trust. Robert made it a point to practice what he preached. If he advocated for work-life balance, he ensured he took his own advice and didn't send late-night emails or set unrealistic expectations.

Recognizing and appreciating others' contributions is also vital. Acknowledging the efforts and achievements of others fosters a positive and trusting environment. When people feel valued for their work, their trust in leadership and the organization deepens. Robert regularly celebrated team milestones and individual accomplishments, making everyone feel seen and appreciated.

Trust is also maintained through fairness and impartiality. Treating everyone with equal respect and without favoritism builds a culture of trust. When people see that rules and expectations apply to everyone equally, their trust in the system and its leaders is reinforced. Robert ensured that all team members had equal opportunities for growth and development, applying policies consistently and fairly.

Adapting to change while maintaining core values is another aspect of sustaining trust. Change is inevitable, but how it is managed can either strengthen or weaken trust. Being adaptable and resilient while staying true to core values shows that you are reliable even in uncertain times. During periods of organizational change, Robert kept his team informed, addressed their concerns, and remained steadfast in his commitment to their professional growth and well-being.

Long-term trust also involves investing in relationships. Building strong, personal connections with team members goes beyond daily tasks and projects. It involves showing genuine interest in their lives and aspirations. Robert made an effort to know his team members on a personal level, celebrating their successes outside of work and supporting them through challenges. This personal investment made the professional bond stronger and trust more enduring.

Finally, fostering a culture of trust within the team or organization amplifies individual efforts. When trust is a shared value and embedded in the culture, it becomes self-reinforcing. This involves encouraging team members to trust each other and providing opportunities for team-building and collaboration. Robert facilitated team-building activities and created spaces for informal interaction, which helped the team members build mutual trust. He also encouraged a culture of open feedback, where team members could share their thoughts and concerns without fear of retribution.

Chapter 5

Emotional Intelligence in Communication

Understanding Emotional Intelligence

Emotional intelligence (EI) is a pivotal skill that influences every facet of life, from personal relationships to professional success. It encompasses the ability to recognize, understand, and manage our own emotions, as well as the capacity to recognize, understand, and influence the emotions of others. Mastering emotional intelligence can lead to better decision-making, improved relationships, and greater well-being.

Imagine you're navigating a complex project at work. The deadlines are tight, and stress levels are high. Colleagues are on edge, and the pressure is palpable. In such a scenario, emotional intelligence becomes a critical asset. It enables you to stay calm, assess the situation objectively, and respond thoughtfully rather than reacting impulsively.

One key component of emotional intelligence is self-awareness. This involves being in tune with your own emotions as they arise. Recognizing how you feel in the moment can prevent you from being overwhelmed by your emotions or acting out of impulse. For example, if you notice yourself becoming frustrated during a meeting, you can take a moment to pause, breathe, and reflect on why you're feeling that way. This self-awareness allows you to manage your emotions and maintain composure, even under pressure.

Self-regulation is another crucial aspect of emotional intelligence. It's about controlling your emotional responses and staying adaptable in the face of change. People who are skilled in self-regulation don't let their emotions dictate their actions. Instead, they use their awareness to manage their reactions constructively. For instance, if a project hits an unexpected snag, rather than reacting with panic or anger, someone with strong self-regulation skills will calmly assess the situation and develop a plan to address the issue.

Motivation, particularly intrinsic motivation, is also a significant part of emotional intelligence. This means having a passion for what you do that goes beyond external rewards like money or status. Intrinsically motivated individuals are driven by internal factors such as personal growth, the pursuit of knowledge, or the desire to achieve a meaningful goal. This internal drive can help you stay focused and resilient, even when faced with setbacks. For example, a teacher who is intrinsically motivated will continue to strive for excellence in their teaching methods, not just for the sake of a promotion or recognition, but because they genuinely care about their students' success.

Empathy, the ability to understand and share the feelings of others, is another vital element of emotional intelligence. Empathy allows you to build deeper connections with others by seeing the world from their perspective. When you empathize with colleagues, friends, or family members, you create an environment of trust and understanding. For instance, if a co-worker is visibly stressed, an empathetic response would involve acknowledging their feelings and offering support, rather than dismissing their concerns. This kind of empathetic interaction fosters stronger, more collaborative relationships.

Social skills, including effective communication and conflict resolution, round out the components of emotional intelligence. Strong social skills enable you to interact harmoniously with others, navigate social complexities, and build robust networks. Effective communication involves not just speaking clearly but also listening actively. When you truly listen to others, you validate their experiences and build rapport. For example, in a team meeting, practicing active listening by making eye contact, nodding, and summarizing what others have said can help ensure everyone feels heard and valued.

Conflict resolution is another critical social skill. Conflicts are inevitable, but how you handle them can make a significant difference. An emotionally intelligent approach to conflict involves addressing issues directly and constructively, seeking to understand the underlying concerns of all parties involved. For instance, if two team members are at odds over a project direction, an emotionally intelligent leader would facilitate a discussion where both can voice their perspectives, and work together to find a mutually acceptable solution.

Developing emotional intelligence is an ongoing process that requires deliberate practice and reflection. One effective strategy is to engage in regular self-reflection, perhaps through journaling or mindfulness practices. Reflecting on your emotional responses to various situations can help you understand your triggers and patterns, making it easier to manage your emotions in the future.

Another practical approach is to seek feedback from others. Constructive feedback can provide valuable insights into how your emotions and behaviors impact those around you. For example, you might ask a trusted colleague to observe your interactions and provide feedback on your communication style or emotional responses. This external perspective can help you identify areas for improvement that you might not have noticed on your own.

Developing empathy can be enhanced by actively practicing perspective-taking. This involves making a conscious effort to understand the emotions and viewpoints of others. You can practice this by engaging in conversations with a genuine interest in learning about the other person's experiences and feelings. Asking open-ended questions, such as "How did that situation make you feel?" or "What's your perspective on this issue?" can encourage deeper, more empathetic discussions.

Improving social skills often involves stepping out of your comfort zone and engaging in new social interactions. This could mean taking on leadership roles, participating in team-building activities, or simply making an effort to connect with colleagues or peers on a personal level. These interactions provide valuable opportunities to practice and refine your communication and conflict-resolution skills in real-world settings.

Recognizing and Managing Your Emotions

Recognizing and managing your emotions is a crucial skill that can significantly impact both your personal and professional life. Emotions influence how we think, act, and interact with others. Being aware of your emotions and knowing how to manage them can lead to better decision-making, healthier relationships, and greater emotional well-being.

Consider a typical morning when you're rushing to get to work on time. The alarm didn't go off, you're running late, and to top it off, you spill coffee on your shirt. The frustration builds, and by the time you get to the office, you're irritable and short with your colleagues. This scenario highlights the importance of recognizing your emotions. If you had acknowledged your frustration early on, you might have taken a few moments to calm down, preventing the negative impact on your day and your interactions with others.

Self-awareness is the foundation of emotional management. It involves being conscious of your emotions as they occur. This awareness allows you to understand the triggers and patterns in your emotional responses. Start by regularly checking in with yourself. Throughout the day, pause and ask, "How am I feeling right now?" Identifying your emotions—whether it's anger, sadness, joy, or anxiety—is the first step toward managing them effectively.

Once you recognize an emotion, the next step is to understand it. Reflect on what caused this feeling. Was it an external event, like a disagreement with a colleague, or an internal trigger, such as a negative thought? Understanding the root cause of your emotions can help you address them more effectively. For instance, if you realize that a tight deadline is causing your stress, you can take proactive steps to manage your workload better.

Managing your emotions doesn't mean suppressing them. Instead, it's about finding healthy ways to express and cope with them. One effective strategy is to practice mindfulness. Mindfulness involves staying present in the moment and observing your thoughts and feelings without judgment. By doing so, you create a space between the emotion and your reaction, allowing you to choose a more considered response.

Breathing exercises are a simple yet powerful mindfulness technique. When you feel overwhelmed by an emotion, take a few deep breaths. Focus on the sensation of the breath entering and leaving your body. This practice can help calm your mind and reduce the intensity of your emotions. For example, if you're feeling anxious before a big presentation, spending a few minutes on deep breathing can help you regain composure and confidence.

Journaling is another effective tool for managing emotions. Writing about your feelings can provide clarity and insight. It allows you to process your emotions and explore their underlying causes. Set aside a few minutes each day to write about your experiences and how they made you feel. Over time, you may notice patterns in your emotional responses, which can help you develop strategies to manage them better.

Consider the story of John, a project manager known for his high-stress levels. John often found himself reacting angrily to setbacks, which strained his relationships with his team. Realizing the need for change, John started journaling about his emotional experiences. Through this practice, he identified that his anger was often triggered by fear of failure. With this insight, John began to address his fear directly, setting more realistic goals and developing a healthier perspective on setbacks. As a result, his emotional reactions became more balanced, and his relationships improved.

Another essential aspect of managing emotions is developing emotional resilience. Emotional resilience is the ability to adapt to stressful situations and bounce back from adversity. Building resilience involves cultivating a positive outlook, maintaining a support network, and practicing self-care.

Positive self-talk can significantly influence your emotional resilience. Replace negative, self-defeating thoughts with more positive and constructive ones. For instance, if you catch yourself thinking, "I'll never get this right," reframe it to, "This is challenging, but I can learn and improve." This shift in mindset can help you approach difficulties with a more resilient attitude.

Maintaining strong connections with friends, family, and colleagues provides emotional support during tough times. Don't hesitate to reach out to your support network when you're feeling overwhelmed. Talking about your feelings with someone you trust can provide relief and perspective. For example, sharing your frustrations with a close friend can help you feel understood and less isolated.

Self-care practices are vital for emotional management. Regular exercise, a balanced diet, adequate sleep, and time for relaxation all contribute to emotional well-being. When your body is well-cared for, you're better equipped to handle emotional challenges. For example, taking a walk or practicing yoga can help reduce stress and improve your mood.

In the workplace, managing emotions is crucial for maintaining a positive and productive environment. Effective communication is key to managing emotions in professional settings. When you feel a strong emotion, take a moment to compose yourself before responding. Use "I" statements to express your feelings without blaming others. For instance, instead of saying, "You always ignore my ideas," you could say, "I feel frustrated when my ideas aren't considered."

Conflict resolution skills are also essential for managing emotions at work. Approach conflicts with a problem-solving mindset rather than an adversarial one. Listen actively to the other person's perspective and seek common ground. By focusing on finding a solution rather than winning an argument, you can manage your emotions and maintain professional relationships.

Empathy: The Key to Understanding Others

Empathy is the key to understanding others, an essential skill that fosters connection, compassion, and cooperation in both personal and professional relationships. It enables you to step into another person's shoes, see the world from their perspective, and respond with genuine care and concern. By cultivating empathy, you can improve communication, resolve conflicts more effectively, and build stronger, more meaningful connections.

Imagine you're working with a colleague, Alex, on a critical project. As the deadline approaches, tensions rise, and Alex seems increasingly stressed and irritable. Instead of reacting defensively to Alex's behavior, you take a moment to consider what might be causing their stress. You remember that Alex recently mentioned having difficulty balancing work and family responsibilities. By acknowledging this, you decide to approach Alex with empathy rather than frustration. You say, "I've noticed you seem quite stressed lately. Is there anything I can do to help lighten the load?" This empathetic approach can open a dialogue, reduce tension, and foster a more collaborative working environment.

To develop empathy, start with active listening. This means fully focusing on the speaker, understanding their message, responding thoughtfully, and remembering what was said. Active listening goes beyond hearing words; it involves paying attention to non-verbal cues such as facial expressions, body language, and tone of voice. These cues often reveal more about a person's feelings than words alone.

For instance, during a team meeting, you notice that Maria, usually vocal and engaged, is unusually quiet and withdrawn. Instead of assuming she's uninterested, you might observe her body language and facial expressions, which suggest she's upset. After the meeting, you could say, "Maria, I noticed you were quieter than usual in the meeting. Is everything okay?" This shows you're attuned to her emotional state and care about her well-being, which can encourage her to open up and share her concerns.

Another crucial aspect of empathy is withholding judgment. People's experiences and reactions are shaped by their unique backgrounds, cultures, and personal histories. When you approach others without preconceived notions, you create a safe space for honest communication. For example, if a friend confides in you about a mistake they made, responding with empathy rather than judgment can make a significant difference. You might say, "That sounds really tough. I'm here for you if you need to talk about it," rather than, "I can't believe you did that." This empathetic response validates their feelings and encourages them to share more openly.

Empathy also involves recognizing and respecting the emotions of others, even if you don't fully understand or agree with them. This can be particularly challenging in conflict situations. Suppose you're in a disagreement with a partner about how to spend your weekend. Rather than insisting on your preference, try to understand their perspective. You might say, "I see that you really want to visit your family this weekend. Can you help me understand why it's so important to you?" This approach not only shows respect for their feelings but also opens the door to finding a compromise that satisfies both parties.

Empathy can be especially powerful in leadership. A leader who practices empathy can inspire loyalty and motivate their team. Consider Jane, a manager who leads a diverse team with varying needs and challenges. Jane makes a point to regularly check in with her team members, not just about work but about their overall well-being. When one team member, Sam, struggles with a family illness, Jane offers flexible working hours to accommodate Sam's needs. This empathetic gesture not only helps Sam manage their personal situation but also fosters a sense of trust and commitment within the team.

In addition to interpersonal relationships, empathy plays a vital role in customer relations. Businesses that understand and respond to their customers' needs and emotions can build stronger, more loyal customer bases. For example, if a customer expresses frustration about a product issue, responding with empathy can turn a negative experience into a positive one.